Speaking for Yourself

As a student, and in any profession based on your studies, you need good oral communication skills. It is therefore extremely important to develop your ability to converse, to discuss, to argue persuasively, and to speak in public. This is one reason why, whatever subject you study, you will be encouraged to discuss your work in seminars and you will have opportunities to give short talks or presentations.

Most people probably take for granted their ability to speak, not thinking much about it until they have to address an audience or attend an important interview. However, just as your first impressions of other people are based on how they look and how they speak – so are their impressions of you. In every conversation, as well as when you give a talk or presentation, or are interviewed, you are not only conveying information about the subject being discussed but also presenting yourself.

Speaking for Yourself provides clear, straightforward advice that will help you:

- be a good listener
- express yourself clearly and persuasively
- contribute effectively to discussions
- prepare talks or presentations
- prepare effective visual aids
- deliver effective presentations
- perform well in interviews

In short, it will help you to express your thoughts clearly and persuasively – and so to achieve your short-term and medium term   nd your career goals.

Robert Barrass has many years' exp   e and diploma courses at the Univer   ir writing and other key skills. His othei   s, also published by Routledge, include   ̨ ̨uiue to better *Writing in Coursework and Examinations* and *Study! A Guide to Effective Learning, Revision and Examination Techniques*.

Speaking for Yourself
A guide for students

Robert Barrass

Routledge
Taylor & Francis Group

LONDON AND NEW YORK

First published 2006
by Routledge
2 Park Square, Milton Park, Abingdon, Oxon OX14 4RN

Simultaneously published in the USA and Canada
by Routledge
270 Madison Ave, New York, NY 10016

Routledge is an imprint of the Taylor & Francis Group

© 2006 Robert Barrass

Typeset in Goudy by
Keystroke, Jacaranda Lodge, Wolverhampton
Printed and bound in Great Britain by
TJ International Ltd, Padstow, Cornwall

British Library Cataloguing in Publication Data
A catalogue record for this book is available from the British Library

Library of Congress Cataloging in Publication Data
A catalog record for this book has been applied for

ISBN10: 0–415–37856–7 (hbk)
ISBN10: 0–415–37857–5 (pbk)

ISBN13: 9–78–0–415–37856–7 (hbk)
ISBN13: 9–78–0–415–37857–4 (pbk)

Contents

Figures and tables

Figures

Tables

Preface

The ability to communicate one's thoughts clearly, concisely and convincingly – in speaking and in writing – is a key skill in study and in any career based on a college or university education. Yet, although many try to improve their written work, most students give little thought to developing their oral communication skills – until they have to attend their first tutorial, introduce a subject in a seminar, or prepare and deliver a short talk or presentation.

I hope *Speaking for Yourself* will encourage students to think more about what they say and how they say it in all serious conversations and discussions, as well as when they have to attend an interview or address an audience. I hope it will help both those who recognise that they have difficulty in putting their thoughts into words and those who, although they speak confidently, are prepared to consider the possibility of improvement. I also hope that experienced speakers who refer to any page will read there the kind of straightforward common-sense advice that they themselves would give to a student – and which is needed even by some experienced speakers if only they were prepared to consider the possibility of improvement.

In short, I hope *Speaking for Yourself* will help you to ensure that your spoken words work for you – helping you to achieve your short-term, medium-term and career goals. If you are just starting at college or university, I suggest that you read it, perhaps one chapter at a time early in your course, and then refer to it for guidance on particular points as the need arises. The exercises headed *Improve your performance*, at the end of most chapters, may be undertaken by students working alone or used by tutors in their courses on communication skills.

Acknowledgements

Speaking for Yourself, like my two other books on key skills for students, *Study!* and *Students Must Write*, is based on my experience: as a student and as an administrator and lecturer in several colleges and universities – but mainly in helping students on degree and diploma courses at the University of Sunderland to develop their key skills. In preparing this new book, I have been helped by Mark Davies and Anne Cunningham of the School of Health, Natural and Social Sciences, and Robert Jewitt of the School of Arts, Design, Media and Culture, who reviewed parts of the typescript, and by Jane Moore of the University of Sunderland's Murray Library, who helped with the chapter on information retrieval. I also thank Les Davison for advice on video conferences, both Norman Catcherside and Trevor Hartley for IT support, Jonathan Barrass for advice on the use of computers in preparing presentations, and Ann, my wife, for her interest, for encouragement, and for help with library research, with the preparation of the typescript, and with proof correction.

Robert Barrass
Sunderland
28 July 2005

1 Speaking for yourself

Good communication skills are needed in everyday life, in study at college or university, and in any career based on such studies. Yet, after more than twelve years at school, many students entering higher education are unable to express their thoughts clearly and effectively in their own language. They need to improve their writing and to develop their ability to converse, to discuss, to argue persuasively, and to speak in public. Indeed, employers complain that after a further three years in college or university, many students applying for employment still have poor communication skills.

Recognising that many school leavers need to improve their communication skills (and to develop other interpersonal skills needed for success in study and in any profession), all courses in further and higher education are intended to facilitate both learning and personal development (see Table 1.1). As a student, therefore, you will receive comments and advice on your written work to help you to improve your writing, and you will have opportunities to discuss your work and to give short talks or presentations. That is to say, you will be encouraged to develop your ability to express your thoughts effectively.

Most people probably take for granted their ability to speak, not thinking much about it until they have to address an audience or attend an important interview. But just as your first impressions of other people are based on how they look and how they speak – so are their impressions of you. Every time you speak, not just when giving a talk or being interviewed, you are both conveying information relevant to the subject being discussed and presenting yourself.

When you meet people for the first time their immediate feelings about you, based on your appearance and behaviour, are important both at the time and later – because they are not easily forgotten or revised. You never have a second opportunity to make a good first impression; and those people whom you meet only once may never have further evidence of your character and ability.

Table 1.1 Some skills needed in studying any subject and in any career*

Personal skills	Why some students under-achieve
1 Self management	Not working hard enough, poorly directed effort. Overwork. Problems with relationships.
2 Money management	Worries about money.
3 Time management	Ineffective use of time for study, recreation and rest.
4 Summarising	Inability to distinguish important points from the supporting detail, and to make good notes.
5 Finding information	Not making good use of libraries and other sources of ideas and information.
6 Processing information	Not bringing together relevant information and ideas from lectures, tutorials, seminars, practical work, background reading and other sources.
7 Problem solving	Not thinking things through to a satisfactory conclusion.
8 Thinking and creativity	Mindless repetition of other people's thoughts: unwillingness to consider new approaches or different points of view.
9 Communicating	Not expressing thoughts clearly, concisely and persuasively when speaking or in writing.

Note
* Based on Barrass *Study!* (2001).

Your appearance and speech may create barriers between you and the people you meet, or may help them to feel at ease in your presence. From your speech people make assumptions, which may or may not be correct, about your place of birth and social class (from your pronunciation), about your education (from whether or not you express your thoughts clearly), about your interests and opinions (from what you say), and about your intelligence (from whether or not what you say seems to make good sense).

When you speak, you know what you are thinking and how you feel about it; and as you speak other people make judgements about your character and assumptions about what you are thinking and why: first from your appearance, and then from *how you speak* and from *what you say* (see Figure 1.1). As people come to know you better they also judge you by *what you do* – by your actions, which speak louder than words: they make clear whether or not you meant what you said.

WORDS SPOKEN

EYE CONTACTS and FACIAL EXPRESSIONS

POSITION POSTURE GESTURES

INTEREST and AWARENESS

BACKGROUND and PRIOR KNOWLEDGE

FIXED OPINIONS and PREJUDICES

PREFERENCES and LOYALTIES

MOTIVES and HIDDEN AGENDAS

ATTITUDES and BELIEFS

PREOCCUPATIONS

UNDERSTANDING

THOUGHTS

Figure 1.1   Verbal and non-verbal communication; thoughts and feelings. There is much more to an iceberg than meets the eye of a seafarer. Similarly, our behaviour, which others perceive in face-to-face conversations, provides clues to what is below the surface: to our thoughts and feelings, and to why we are as we are.

How you speak

We are remarkably sensitive to the vocal characteristics of speech, as indicated by our ability to recognise the voices of many people whom we hear only in telephone conversations or on the radio. We also notice other characteristics of the way people speak. If they are considerate, in any serious conversation or discussion we expect brevity, clarity, sincerity and politeness. From such clues, when speaking on the telephone or listening to the radio, we may form an impression of a person's character – which may or may not be correct. In face-to-face conversations we are more confident in our ability to judge people from the way they speak.

Be brief

Even if listeners are interested in what you are saying, they will expect you to come to the point quickly. In a presentation, ten minutes with one person talking is long enough. That is why experienced speakers, especially in longer talks, use facial expressions and gestures as well as words, and include visual aids, demonstrations, samples, specimens and handouts, as appropriate, and perhaps ask rhetorical questions, so that people do not have to sit and listen for more than a few minutes to just one person speaking.

Radio and television producers require a listener to have only a very short attention span. Many news programmes have two news readers or presenters, and neither they nor the other contributors speak for more than a few seconds at a time. Similarly, in everyday conversations and discussions most people speak briefly and to the point. All participants are stimulated by the variety of contributions and are likely to feel involved.

Be clear

Think before you speak

Clarity in a formal talk, presentation or speech, as in writing, depends on choosing words that both you and your audience understand (see chapter 4 *Choosing the right word*) and on expressing your thoughts in carefully considered and properly constructed sentences (see chapter 5 *Using words effectively*). In conversation it is not usually possible to achieve such clarity because, instead of thinking and planning before attempting to communicate, you have to think as you speak, and while others are speaking.

Conversation and discussion help to clarify your thoughts and contribute to your own knowledge and understanding of any subject, as does all the work that goes into your preparation of an essay or written report. So you are likely to be in a better position to talk or to write with clarity about the subject at the end of any conversation or discussion than you were at the beginning.

Know your subject

Before explaining things to others, you must ensure that you have sufficient knowledge and understanding yourself. Then you must consider how best to explain. As a result, conversation and discussion may be part of your preparations before you give a talk or presentation, as they are before you write an essay or report.

Use appropriate language

In higher education and in most careers, to be widely understood when speaking, as well as choosing words that they expect everyone present to understand, most people use standard English words and standard pronunciation (also called received pronunciation because it is widely understood). Those who use slang (highly colloquial language, including words that are not included in the vocabulary of most educated English-speaking people, and words used in a special sense different from their commonly accepted meaning) will not be so widely understood.

For example, unless you were born in north-east England, you might not understand every word of the anonymous tragic ballad about 'The Lambton Worm' (a dragon), especially if the singer had a strong Wearside accent. It begins:

> Whisht lads, haad yer gobs
> Aal tell ye aall an aafu' story
> Whisht lads, haad yer gobs,
> Aal tell ye boot the warm.

This means, in standard English: 'Quiet, everyone, while I tell you this story, full of awe, about the worm.'

If you use standard English (as used in quality English-language newspapers in the British Isles and elsewhere), choose words that convey your meaning accurately, arrange them in carefully constructed unambiguous sentences, and pronounce each word correctly (using standard English pronunciation, as explained in a good dictionary), you will be understood by English-speaking people everywhere.

Pronounce each word carefully

Whatever you are trying to achieve, you must articulate carefully and speak so that everyone present hears every word. On a formal occasion, as in an interview or when delivering a talk or presentation, it is best to use standard English; but if appropriate on a less formal occasion, as in everyday conversations and discussions, you may prefer to use a more colloquial language (see pages 54 and 75). But clear articulation is always necessary, in addition to the clarity that results from care in the choice and use of words.

Be sincere

By convention a personal letter ends with the complimentary close 'Yours sincerely' or 'Yours truly', affirming that you believe what you have said to be true. In any serious conversation it should not be necessary to say that you are sincere; but for your words to carry conviction – in standard or colloquial English – your voice must sound sincere, and in face-to-face conversations or when addressing an audience you must look sincere.

Most people find it easiest to maintain eye contact when they are telling the truth, and may look away when they are not. However, a person's sincerity cannot be assessed by eye contact alone, and a listener who has to cope with rather too much eye contact may suspect that a speaker is insincere – and trying too hard! Similarly, a person who is sincere does not gain credibility by using superfluous introductory phrases that indicate to listeners that the speaker does not always tell the truth (see Table 1.2).

There are of course many occasions when it is not possible to tell the truth, perhaps to avoid breaking a confidence or to avoid giving offence. Then it is important that one should not tell lies, because of the loss of confidence and credibility later when lies are detected. You may be able to avoid telling lies about other people by saying that you cannot answer for them: that you cannot affirm or deny any statement, or discuss any rumour concerning their affairs. Otherwise, as in the game 'Twenty Questions' (in which the answer to each question must be either yes or no), a questioner will soon obtain relevant facts by a process of elimination.

Table 1.2 Some introductory phrases to avoid

Introductory phrase	Meaning?
To be honest . . .	I don't always tell the truth.
As is well known . . .	I expect you know this.
It is common knowledge that . . .	I am not going to explain this.
It can safely be said that . . .	In my opinion . . .
It is perhaps true to say that . . .	I don't know what to think.
All right-minded people think . . .	If you disagree with me, you're wrong.
Most independent observers would agree.	I think some people agree with me.
All reasonable people think . . .	I believe . . .
I genuinely believe . . .	I believe . . .
To be absolutely frank . . .	This is what I really think.
As a matter of fact, there is no . . .	There is no . . .
With respect, there is no . . .	I disagree, there is no. . . .

Be polite

The usual greeting when meeting someone for the first time is to say 'How do you do' or, less formally, 'Hello'. Then, to end this first conversation, if appropriate you could say 'It has been a pleasure to meet you.' More important, you should look as if your meeting has been a pleasure.

When meeting someone whom you know well, a common greeting is 'How are you?'. This greeting is not an invitation to recite your medical history or to provide an up-date on your state of health.

In any conversation, you are most likely to persuade others, or to obtain their agreement, co-operation and support, if you are obviously interested and considerate: (a) if your manner is friendly; (b) if you address individuals by name; (c) if you smile when you meet; (d) if you consult them at least on occasions when they should be consulted; and (e) if you agree with them when you can.

Special care is needed when you speak on the telephone, unless it is a video call, because there is no non-verbal communication. So, whatever else you say, always: (a) begin your conversation with your name; (b) use the name of the person you are calling; and (c) end, if appropriate, by saying 'Thank you for your help'.

Etiquette, which may be taught as a set of rules, is a guide to acceptable behaviour in polite society – helping those in Rome to do as Romans do. Good manners in conversation, as in any other social interaction, are no more than common sense: showing one's respect, interest and pleasure or, at least, ensuring that one does not give offence.

> And certainly the greatest asset [one] can have is charm. And charm cannot exist without good manners – meaning by this, not so much manners that precisely follow particular rules, as manners that have been made smooth and polished by the continuous practice of kind impulses.
>
> *Etiquette*, Emily Post (1942)

Then tact depends not so much on saying the right things at the right time as on knowing what you should not say, including an awareness of topics that are best avoided.

When speaking, as with other aspects of behaviour, there are socially accepted notions as to what is and what is not appropriate in particular circumstances. For example, you might be expected: (a) to respond to a greeting with a similar greeting – and a smile; (b) to be co-operative, responding to a request either by agreeing to help or by explaining why you are unable to help; or (c) when asked 'Would you like . . . ?' to reply, with a smile, either 'Yes please' or 'No thank you'.

In any conversation or discussion you must listen carefully to the contributions of others and have the confidence to contribute yourself. That is to say, you should listen without being submissive. Normally, you should be assertive, ensuring that your message is clearly expressed and understood (see *Be forceful*, page 39), but you should not be aggressive (for example, you should not attempt to dominate by speaking loudly or by using language intended to ridicule the views of others).

Abusive language, comprising words intended to offend the person addressed, is unacceptable – as are gestures intended to insult the person against whom they are directed. Such abuse, and the use of words or phrases that could give offence to anyone who differs from the speaker in age, appearance, race, religion or sexual orientation, are to be avoided in all conversations, discussions, talks or presentations – as a student and, after graduation, in any profession. Similarly, one should never say anything that is false or defamatory (scandalous) or anything likely to cause anyone to be shunned or avoided, or exposed to hatred, ridicule or contempt.

What is socially acceptable in conversation will depend on who is present, and on the place, the time and the occasion. Care is necessary not only in ensuring that your own conduct and use of words are appropriate but also in observing and interpreting non-verbal clues to the feelings of others. Even something as fundamental as a smile may be misunderstood by people whom you know well: it is not necessarily a spontaneous expression of pleasure; and laughter may indicate amusement, discomfort, embarrassment, surprise, wonder or . . . There are also cultural differences in expectations relating, for example, to the need for personal space and to the use or avoidance of eye contact (see BBC, 2005) which if not understood can easily cause discomfort or annoyance.

What you say

Be accurate

You may know the party game in which people sit in a circle, and one whispers a message to a neighbour, and then says 'Pass it on'. All each person has to do is listen carefully and pass on the message. There would be nothing of interest in this game if each person listened carefully, remembered the message exactly, and whispered clearly – repeating it word for word. But usually this does not happen, and by the time the message comes round to the originator it is inaccurate and may have changed so much as to be amusing. The more people there are in the circle, the more it is likely to differ from the original.

In other situations, failure to pass on messages accurately is likely to have serious and even fatal consequences (for example, inaccurate messages may result in a waste of time in any business, in a loss of production in industry, or in a failure to respond appropriately when first aid is required urgently immediately after an accident). This game can therefore be used in courses on communication skills as the basis for a class exercise. It can also be used when training first aid workers, for example, to emphasise the care needed to ensure clarity and accuracy when passing messages by word of mouth.

Communication is complex, even when speaking to someone directly, face to face or on the telephone, or when sending a written message. It is not easy to ensure that you have expressed your meaning adequately or that you will be understood (see Figure 1.2).

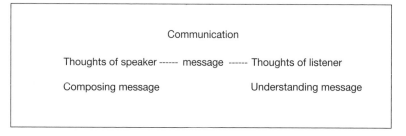

Figure 1.2 Accurate communication, using words alone, is not easy. Verbal communication involves your choosing words and using them to convey your thoughts accurately as an unambiguous message – in an attempt to evoke identical thoughts in the minds of listeners or readers, so that they understand your message correctly.

In verbal communication (when transferring information using words alone, as in a letter or an e-mail, or when speaking on the telephone to someone you cannot see), you (the sender) put your thoughts into words so that they can be sent as a message – in an attempt to provoke identical thoughts in the mind of a reader or listener (the receiver). This involves care on the part of the sender, who must: (a) consider what the receiver needs to know and why this information is needed; (b) convey just this information as a message, with enough supporting detail; (c) choose words the receiver is expected to know and understand; and (d) use these words correctly in well-constructed unambiguous sentences.

Care is also necessary on the part of the receiver, who must pay attention both to the words used and, in speech especially, to the way they are expressed. Then the interpretation of the message is influenced by the receiver's prior knowledge, likes and dislikes, opinions and beliefs, and in face-to-face conversations, discussions and talks, by the accompanying non-verbal signals.

Whether or not people are actually speaking, information transfer is facilitated by unspoken clues to their thoughts and feelings (see Figure 1.1). This non-verbal communication (involving position, posture, eye contact, facial expressions and other gestures) is aptly called body language. It reinforces the words used but is more fundamental than speech and sometimes makes words unnecessary. For example, if in conversation our eyebrows do not move they reveal nothing of our thoughts; if raised slightly they indicate *surprise*; if raised fully, *disbelief*; if lowered slightly, *puzzlement*; if lowered fully, *anger*. So, although we learn to control the outward expression of our emotions to some extent, in face-to-face conversations and discussions we cannot always avoid revealing unspoken thoughts and feelings that we might prefer to keep to ourselves.

Be appropriate

To capture and hold attention, what you say (content) and how you say it (arrangement and delivery) must be appropriate to your purpose, to your subject, to the needs of your audience, and to the occasion. So always check, if you can, that any assumptions you make about these things are correct; as does Martin Chuzzlewit, soon after meeting Tom Pinch:

> 'If you like punch, you'll allow me to order a glass apiece . . . that we may usher in our friendship in a becoming manner. To let you into a secret, Mr Pinch, I never was so much in want of something warm and cheering in my life; but I didn't like to run the chance of being found drinking it, without knowing what kind of person you were; for first impressions, you know, often go a long way, and last a long time.'
>
> *Martin Chuzzlewit*, Charles Dickens (1884)

Your purpose in speaking may be, for example, to inform, to convince, to consult, to provide feedback, to review, to agree a course of action, to instruct, to introduce a discussion, to question, to find fault, or to praise. Your purpose will influence your choice of words, your use of eye contact, your facial expressions and gestures, the position you adopt in relation to your audience, and perhaps also the way you dress and where you choose to speak.

As to the subject, to the needs of your audience and to the occasion, if you were talking to people who had invited you to speak about flowers you would talk only about flowers – *ensuring relevance*. However, you might talk, for example: to students of biology about a flower's structure and the functions of its parts; to flower growers about methods of cultivation, consumer demand and packaging; to florists about how to care for flowers and display them for sale; to historians about the significance of flowers as emblems of political parties and of warring factions; and to artists about shape and colour, about representing flowers in embroidery and tapestry, and about famous artists whose names are associated with particular flowers.

What you do

What do you admire most in others (for example, that they are able, concerned, conscientious, considerate, enthusiastic, fair minded, flexible, genuine, honest, open, sincere, trustworthy)? Whose advice would you seek to help you make balanced judgements?

As to credibility, Aristotle 384–322 BC considered that persuasion is achieved first by the speaker's personal character; second by the effect of the words used when they stir the emotions; and third by persuasive arguments suitable to the case in question (Ross, 1946).

When you promise to do something, do you remember to do it? Those who come to know you will respect you for what you say, and how you say it, only if they find that you are consistent: that you do say what you mean, and that your actions do support your words.

> All the virtues of language are, in their roots, moral; it becomes accurate if the speaker desires to be true; clear, if he speaks with sympathy and a desire to be intelligible; powerful, if he has earnestness; pleasant, if he has a sense of rhythm and order. There are no other virtues of language producible by art than these.
>
> (John Ruskin quoted in Sampson, 1925: 70)

Improve your performance

Use standard English – a world language

The standardisation of English

William Cobbett, a political journalist, considered a knowledge of grammar as a weapon in the struggle of the working classes against their oppressors and hoped that his *Grammar of the English Language*, published in both America and England in 1819, would help the common people (apprentices, ploughboys, soldiers, sailors) to learn for themselves the things necessary for their salvation. Similarly, the Elementary Education Act of 1870 was intended to ensure that all children in the United Kingdom left school able to read and to express themselves clearly in their own language.

Fifty years later, the report of a government committee of inquiry into the teaching of English asserted that the first duty of those providing an elementary education was to give all its pupils speech and that 'The accomplishment of clear and correct speech is the definite accomplishment children are entitled to demand . . . so that they can speak clearly and with expression to other English speaking people, and to those who use English as a second language' (Newbolt, 1921). In *English for the English* (1925), Sampson, a member of the Newbolt Committee, regretted that education authorities in England did not seem to recognise the importance of clear speech, as the foundation both for writing good English and for the study of all other subjects.

In the preface to his play *Pygmalion* (1916), George Bernard Shaw had emphasised the importance of clear speech: 'The English have no respect for their language, and will not teach their children to speak it. . . . It is impossible for an Englishman to open his mouth without making some other Englishman despise him.' This opinion is well known from A. J. Lerner's lyric 'Why can't the English teach their children how to speak?' in *My Fair Lady*, the A. J. Lerner and F. Loewe 1956 musical version of *Pygmalion*.

Another government inquiry into the teaching of English, meeting fifty years after the Newbolt Committee, again emphasised the importance of clear speech as the basis for the study of all school subjects and for adult life:

> The sixteen year old pupil . . . should be able to speak his own mind, to write what he is taught, and to have care for the correctness of spoken English. He should be able to understand what he reads and hears, master ideas, and re-state them in his own way.
>
> A *Language for Life*, Bullock (1975)

The merits of standard English

In spite of this recognition of the importance of clear speech, there has been a change in many people's attitude to standard spoken English. For example, whereas the adults presenting radio programmes for children in the first half of the twentieth century used standard spoken English (standard English words and received pronunciation – known then as BBC English), by the end of the century the presenters of BBC radio programmes were no longer required to conform to this standard (Burchfield, 1981). Indeed, many of those presenting programmes for children and teenagers seemed to have been selected because they did not use standard English: perhaps their BBC producers wanted to stimulate interest by providing variety, or perhaps so that (a) children would become familiar with different forms of spoken English; and (b) those children who did not speak standard English at home would sometimes hear on the radio voices similar to their own.

In any career much more time is spent in speaking than in writing; and those who speak fluently are likely also to write fluently. Yet speech is learnt by example, in the home, and those who learn to speak English badly at home may not be corrected in schools: perhaps some parents who themselves speak badly consider there to be nothing wrong with their children's speech, and would resent any attempt to correct it as adverse criticism of their own speech.

Indeed, Crowley (1989) states that: 'the attempt to impose standard English on all children [as proposed in the Newbolt report, and in later reports] was not experienced by its recipients as a mode of enfranchisement [as intended by Cobbett in 1819] but as a form of denial of their own practice that can be interpreted as an example of intolerance and hostility to difference and considered anti-social and unjust.'

Opinions about the merits of received pronunciation are likely to continue to differ widely and to be expressed with acrimony; and no one can say with confidence how the battle will go (Fowler, 1968).

However, the development of standard English is not something that was imposed by authority in the nineteenth and twentieth centuries. On the contrary: (a) the conventions of English grammar have been accepted and adhered to by most educated English speakers since the ninth century; (b) spelling was largely fixed in the eighteenth century, and the influence of spelling upon sounds has been constant and considerable, especially since the passing of the Education Act in 1870 (Potter, 1966); and (c) the standard pronunciation that now exists (Grimson and Ramsaran, 1989) is attributable to the standardisation of written English following the invention of the printing press in the fourteenth century, to the preparation of dictionaries of the English language, to the freer movement of people since the days of stage coaches and sailing ships, and to the introduction of the telephone, radio and television in the nineteenth and twentieth centuries.

English as a world language

When communication between people in different regions was difficult it was natural that isolated speech communities, subject to different influences, should develop in different directions. Now that most educated people have access to books and newspapers, radio and television, mobile phones and the Internet, all educated English-speaking people are familiar with standard English or standard American English. English has become a world language.

Standard English pronunciation (received pronunciation) may still be used by only a minority of the people of Britain (as stated by Fowler, 1968), but it is heard on the radio and television every day and understood by all English-speaking people. It would be unacceptable, therefore, if standard English were not taught by teachers of English in schools, and if poor pronunciation were not corrected by teachers of all subjects. Furthermore, to teach English without teaching the pronunciation of English words would be contrary to the usual practice in teaching other languages.

There are many acceptable varieties of spoken English, but to facilitate international communication anyone learning it as a foreign language needs to know how to pronounce each new word correctly (Baker and Westrup, 2003): each speaker's pronunciation of English words must be understood by other speakers of English. As a result, many people who have learned English as a second language (using a standard English or a standard American pronunciation) can be more widely understood than many who have been taught English in English schools – where teachers are required to start teaching children how to write standard English without first ensuring that both they and their pupils do speak standard English.

Perhaps this is why many English children still speak, read and write badly (have difficulty in communicating in their own language) when they leave school (see Figure 7.2). Twenty-five years after the Bullock inquiry (seventy-five years after the Newbolt inquiry), two more government inquiries, responding to the concerns of employers and others about the communication skills of young people seeking employment, again recommended changes in the teaching of English *and in the training of all teachers* (Kingman, 1988; Dearing, 1997).

Reflect on the importance of good oral communication skills

Whereas in the 1920s employers were complaining about deficiencies in the use of English by 14-year-old school leavers (Newbolt, 1921), before the end of the century they were complaining about the poor English of

16- to 18-year-old school leavers (Bullock, 1975; Kingman, 1988), and of those aged 21 or more, graduating from colleges and universities (Dearing, 1997). Dearing found no consensus among employers as to the main deficiencies (in key skills) of people entering employment after higher education, but about a quarter of the employers consulted complained of inadequate communication skills.

The curriculum for English in schools in England and Wales (DFE, 1995) emphasised that to be effective when speaking and listening at school (and later to participate confidently in public, cultural and working life) pupils should be taught: (a) to use the vocabulary and grammar of standard English, *which they should understand can be expressed in a variety of accents*; (b) to formulate ideas clearly; (c) to speak fluently; (d) to adapt their speech to a widening range of circumstances and demands; and (e) to listen, understand and respond appropriately in conversation.

The ability of school leavers to do these things well should increase their chances of success at college or university – and when applying for employment – and should contribute to their advancement in any career based on academic qualifications.

If employers consider the ability to speak clearly in standard English to be essential, they do not state this clearly when advertising vacancies or in the further particulars sent with their application forms. Instead, in most advertisements for first appointments in administration, business or management, or in the professions, or for advancement in any career, most employers demand good or excellent communication skills. They do not specify which communication skills their employees will need; but it is the appearance and speech of applicants for employment that create the employer's first impression of an interviewee; and employers questioned by Mullen (1997) said: (a) that oral communication was the skill most needed by their employees; and (b) that this skill was sorely lacking in many people they recruited direct from further and higher education in Britain.

So it is appropriate to reflect on your speech and on your ability to converse and discuss. The development of your oral communication skills, supported by sincerity and politeness, is important in study, in any career, and in all your dealings with other people.

2 Conversing

A conversation is an informal interaction involving two or more participants, differing: (a) from a dialogue, which is more formal (as between representatives of the parties to negotiations); (b) from a discussion in a seminar or in a committee meeting, in which agreed rules of procedure are followed; (c) from a talk, presentation or lecture, in which one speaker addresses an audience and may welcome or invite comments and answer questions; and (d) from an interview in which the participants are either interviewing or being interviewed.

In conversation people take turns. They do not say all they would like to say on a subject and then expect others to do the same. Instead, there is an exchange of views. Each person contributes a word, a phrase, a sentence or a few sentences. Anyone speaking for long – without allowing others to have their say – is likely to be considered to be hogging the conversation or being overbearing, or slow to come to the point, rambling or just a bore. If each contribution is brief the conversation is likely to be lively, with everyone paying attention, understanding, and ready to respond.

For a face-to-face conversation, people must be close enough together to hear every word, to maintain eye contact, and to see each participant's facial expressions. If two people in conversation were touching, you might assume that they were greeting one another, or that they were fond of one another, or that one was comforting the other. In most other circumstances people choose not to be too close together. If at a social gathering they may need to stand close together to hear and be heard when groups of people are conversing and there is other background noise. What people feel is a comfortable working distance when they are sitting will depend on such things as how well they know one another and why they are conversing (see Figure 2.1). There are also cultural differences as to what is or is not socially acceptable behaviour, not only in the use of personal space but also in the use of gestures and in the interpretation of facial expressions and other aspects of body language (BBC, 2005).

Personal space

for (A) Conversation   (B) Co-operation   (C) Private study

Figure 2.1   Personal space: two friends sitting at a table, (A) when conversing, (B) when co-operating on a task, and (C) when working independently, share the space in such a way as to facilitate eye contact when conversing, confidential discussion and note-taking when co-operating, and occasional consultation when working on different tasks. Diagrams based on R. Sommer (1965) Further studies of small-group ecology, *Sociometry*, **28**, 337–48. Reprinted in Laver and Hutcheson (1972).

Although there are no rules, it is accepted that each person involved in a serious conversation is present for a purpose and will speak briefly – adding to what others have said so as to move the conversation forward. In taking turns, people choose the right moment to signal their intention to speak, say something that is sequentially relevant (timely and to the point), and then give way to someone else – so that everyone recognises each contribution as being appropriate and everyone has opportunities to speak.

The contributions to a conversation may follow quickly one upon another or may be spaced, depending on such things as the emotional involvement of the participants and their different personalities, and on what is socially acceptable in the setting where the conversation is taking place. As a result, people who meet frequently may converse in a way that has developed as part of their continuing association. Individuals differ as to the length and number of their contributions to any conversation or discussion. People are likely to speak most, and to capture most attention, when speaking about a subject in which they are known to be interested and accepted as being knowledgeable. However, every contribution should be brief, clear, polite and sincere; and every statement should be accurate, relevant and appropriate to both the occasion and the needs of the people present (see *How you speak* (pages 3–8) and *What you say* (pages 8–9).

Your purpose in conversation may be, for example, to seek information, to benefit from the experience of others, or to discuss a problem. As well as speaking yourself, you listen to others, and try to understand and evaluate their words and their non-verbal signals.

In a conversation people take turns, speaking, listening and responding: it is not a conversation if one person is simply giving directions or instructions.

Active listening

In conversation your attention to the contributions of others and your thoughts about what they have said are as important as what you say.

Be attentive

In a simultaneous translation, the translator must: (a) listen to what is said; (b) translate the words spoken into another language; and (c) speak; while (d) listening to and (e) translating what is being said next. You might wonder how the translator is able to do so many things at once.

Yet consider what you do yourself when fully engaged in any conversation or discussion. By paying attention you show that you are present in mind as well as in body. You simultaneously: (a) try to understand what others are saying; (b) appreciate nuances in their voices; (c) maintain sufficient eye contact with them; (d) observe and interpret the posture, facial expressions and other gestures that may indicate their feelings; (e) evaluate their spoken contributions; (f) relate what is said to your own knowledge of the subject and of each speaker, and to your own feelings; (g) provide feedback by responding to what is said with appropriate facial expressions; (h) recognise and record essential points; (i) appreciate when each speaker has made a point and is ready to give way; and (j) are ready, if you wish, to speak yourself.

You must be able to attend to all these things at the same time. If your thoughts are fully occupied with anything that has been said, when others have begun to think and talk about something else, this lapse in attention to what is happening around you may make your further participation in the conversation less effective than it should be.

Lord Chesterfield (1694–1773) advised his son to develop a quickness of attention so as to observe, at once, all the people in a room, their motions, their looks and their words:

> Mind not only what people say, but how they say it; and, if you have any sagacity [quickness of discernment], you may discover more truth by your eyes than by your ears. People can say what they will, but they cannot look just as they will; and their looks frequently discover what their words are calculated to conceal. Therefore, observe people's looks, carefully, when they speak not only to you, but to each other.
>
> *Lord Chesterfield's Letter to His Son*, Roberts (1998)

Without alertness and awareness of everything said in a conversation, and of other people's reactions, you cannot provide appropriate feedback as others speak. Then, when you speak, your words will lack immediacy and relevance. Your absence will be obvious to those who have been paying full attention. They may interpret your words, and your silence when you might have been expected to contribute, as indicating your lack of interest in the topic being discussed or your indifference to their opinions.

If as a result of inattention you do not appreciate all that others have said, you might have to admit that you are unable to answer a direct question because you either did not hear it or are unaware of the context in which it was asked. Worse still, you could fail to do precisely what has been asked of you because you are not sure exactly what is required. Your apparent lack of interest is also likely to result in others being less interested in what you say than they would otherwise have been.

Speaking

Be responsive

Anything you do during a conversation, whether or not you are speaking, is likely to be noticed by other participants – and is likely to influence both their thinking and what they say or do at the time or later. When speaking you convey more information and make your point more forcefully if you make eye contact with each listener than if you rely on words alone. As a result of such non-verbal communication, those involved in a conversation or discussion understand more than is actually said – whereas listeners to a recorded conversation (or readers of contributions to an online discussion, see page 29) can learn only from what was said.

As you listen, you indicate interest not only by looking at other speakers and helping them maintain eye contact, but also by your facial expressions (for example, in conversation by a smile). That is to say, you show your involvement even when you are not speaking, as you do when part of an audience listening to a presentation or talk. As you listen you also appreciate how words are spoken, the speaker's hesitations, the pauses and the silences. You interpret their significance – and may misinterpret them:

> 'But the way I said it must be cleared up. I was unintentionally rude.' . . . A pause in the wrong place, an intonation misunderstood, and a whole conversation went awry. Fielding had been startled, not shocked, but how to convey the difference?
>
> *A Passage to India*, E. M. Forster (1924)

In conversation concise interjections, too short to be interruptions, show not only that you are taking an interest but also, for example, that you do or do not understand, that the speaker has explained sufficiently or that you would like to know more, that you agree or that you are not yet convinced. In market research such short interjections are called sympathetic probes if they simply encourage the speaker to say more (see Table 2.1).

Table 2.1 Interjections: oiling the wheels of conversation

Indicating your interest
   Huha. Hm. Hear, hear! Yes. No. Dear me! Ah. Oh! (ejaculations)
   Is that so! Did they! Really! Would you believe it! (rhetorical questions)

Encouraging the speaker to say more
   You're right. That's true. (indicating agreement)
   I see. I didn't know that. That's interesting. (indicating that you are hearing
      something new)
   I am surprised. (indicating, perhaps, that you are not yet convinced)
   You didn't mention . . .

In contrast, interruptions may break the speaker's train of thought and make it difficult for listeners to concentrate on an argument or explanation. They should be avoided unless urgent clarification is required. For any contribution longer than a helpful interjection, or to ask a timely and urgent question (see Table 2.2), it is polite to await a suitable break in the conversation.

It is possible to make a useful contribution to a conversation without speaking frequently or saying very much. An interesting and informative conversation, enjoyed by all participants, could on analysis be found to have been one-sided. For example, if one person has something interesting to say the full story may unfold in response to sympathetic probing (and direct questioning, see Table 2.2) by a listener who said very little but provided much encouragement. Such an attentive listener could be described as a good listener, and recognised as a good communicator.

You would perhaps enjoy conversing with such a person, and feel at ease. You might feel able to ask questions, discuss a problem, express an opinion, or make suggestions. In short, to be a good conversationalist, you must listen and encourage but you need not talk much yourself – or speak at length.

Table 2.2 Questions and their use in conversation

Direct probes (interjections, as rhetorical questions, that do require an answer)
    You mean . . .
    He said that!

Closed questions (conversation stoppers: can be answered in one word or phrase)
    Do you mean . . . ? Do you agree?
    When did it happen? Who did it? Where were you at the time?

Open questions (requiring more than a yes or no reply)
    Could you explain that again, please? Why was that?
    Could you give an example?
    How did you find out? What happened next?
    What do you think about . . . ?

Leading questions (indicating the answer required, and so best avoided)
    You don't think . . . do you? You wouldn't . . . would you?
    Unacceptable, isn't it? You do agree, don't you!

Improve your performance

Take opportunities to converse

It would be a mistake to think, at any age, that we know all we need to know about conversation. As indicated in this chapter, conversation is remarkably complex social behaviour. Learning the skills involved is part of our continuing education (Laver and Hutcheson, 1972).

One advantage of studying at college or university is that you have opportunities to talk about the subjects you are studying with students whose interests are similar to your own, and to broaden your interests by conversing with people studying other subjects whom you meet if you join any clubs and societies or participate in other social activities. If you live away from home, in student accommodation, this will also give you opportunities to converse with people with backgrounds and interests very different from your own, and to make new friends.

Know what you are trying to achieve

If in conversation you are seeking information, you cannot do better than ask the six questions from Rudyard Kipling's poem 'The Serving Men': 'What? and Why? and When? and How? and Where? and Who?' And if in any conversation, presentation or speech your intention is to convey information, you cannot do better than provide answers to these questions (see pages 31, 73–4, and 88).

Much polite conversation is about everyday concerns and trivial matters that do not require much thought (and are therefore called small talk), but any serious conversation or discussion does require careful thought. Any communication that is inaccurate, inappropriate, imprecise, inconsistent or unclear is likely to be ignored, to confuse, or to result in people making mistakes. So it is necessary to *think*, and then *plan*, before you speak.

Organise your thoughts

Think

Think before you speak. What would you like to achieve? Decide what those listening know already and what they need to know. Consider, for example, their age, education, experience, interests, loyalties, occupations and responsibilities. How are they likely to respond? You will want them all: (a) to understand; and (b) to be affected in a chosen way (for example, to be amused, convinced, encouraged, informed, instructed or persuaded). See also *Consider your purpose*, page 74.

Plan

Decide how best to convey your message.

1   List the points you must make, as they come to mind.
2   Obtain any information needed to fill gaps in your knowledge of the subject.
3   Number the points as you decide how best to begin, how each one leads appropriately to the next, and how to end.
4   Use these notes to remind and guide you as you speak.

Then do not include unnecessary detail. Just make clear what you want to know or to do, or make clear what you would like others to know or to do. Answer any questions concisely.

You will find this procedure helpful before a tutorial, discussion or seminar in which you intend to play an active part, before an interview when you foresee the need to choose your words with care or to speak forcefully on any subject, or before you make a telephone call about anything that is other than routine.

If you know you are to speak for longer on any subject (as when giving a talk or presentation, or leading a discussion) it is best, also, to write in full exactly what you plan to say (see pages 73–4) and then, if you can, to speak from notes (see pages 82–5 and 101–2).

Distinguish between facts and speculation

Consider each of the words listed here (alphabetically, not in order of importance). Some are very similar in meaning, and in a dictionary some are used in explaining the meaning of others in the list, but if you were to write a sentence containing any one of them you would probably find that no other in the list would serve your purpose so well.

Assumption: a statement, based on what we know or believe happened, as to what we think happened later or as to what we expect will happen (our hopes, fears, plans).

Conjecture: guesswork or supposition based on experience, but not proven.

Data: observations recorded and presented as facts, which on analysis yield results.

Expectation: something you think will happen based on previous experience or planning.

Facts: things observed and recorded as data, which are accepted as being true until proved otherwise.

Generalisation: a statement or law based on prior observations or events; that is to say, on what is thought to be true.

Hypothesis: a possible explanation for things observed; or a possible answer to a question, supported by evidence, which may be tested by scientific experiments.

Ideas are what dreams are made of, images in the mind, thoughts and inspirations.

Impression: a thought, less distinct than a notion, which if important you would probably investigate further.

Inference: a statement about the unknown, based on what is known.

Notion: a feeling or inclination relating to observations you cannot understand, and about which you do not have enough evidence to make up your mind.

Opinion: a statement which a speaker or writer believes to be true.

Presumption: something you accept as being correct, based on your knowledge of the subject, but which may not be correct

Rumour: a story in circulation, which may or may not have some foundation in fact.

Speculation: the statement of a hypothesis or theory for which there is evidence but no proof.

Supposition: that which you think, on the basis of evidence and experience.

Surmise: that which you suspect as a result of reasoning from what you know.

Theory: a hypothesis that has stood the test of observation and experiment, and is widely accepted as being probably correct.

Value judgement: a statement of approval or disapproval based on one's own standards.

Keep good records

Making a note

Most students make notes in lectures, but it is just as important to make notes during discussions and seminars, and in any serious conversation. Note-making in study helps you to maintain attention, so that you can recognise and note the important points for immediate attention or for later reference. The recollection of these points, as you write, is also an aid to remembering.

Concise notes, made while you are studying, are an aid to learning; but you will also find that such notes are essential in any career based on your studies. Then, unless you maintain accurate up-to-date records of your work, in appropriate files, there will be times when it is not possible to talk or write with conviction about *what* was said, *what* was to be done, *why* it was necessary, *how* it was done, *who* was involved, and with *what* result.

Notes made during any conversation, discussion or presentation, or while you listen to a longer talk or speech, should comprise abbreviations, numbers, key words, phrases and even whole sentences (for example, conclusions and definitions). Making notes is an aid to concentration, because you have to recognise introductory remarks, examples and digressions so that you can record only main points (perhaps only key words).

Like the notes made in a lecture, those made in any conversation or discussion will serve as personal memoranda – allowing you to attend to what is being said rather than to points already made, relevant to your studies, that you might wish to consider further. If you note points as they are made during a conversation or discussion (that is, make sequential notes) your notes will also be a record of the order in which things were said – and this too may prove to be important later.

Such notes will also be useful, after any important conversation or discussion, when you review your contribution and reflect on what you said, on how you said it, on things said that would perhaps have been better left unsaid, and on whether or not you achieved your objective (for example whether, as a student, you provided or obtained the information required).

In any profession the notes made in conversations and discussions are essential, and anything agreed by the participants must be confirmed in writing. Immediately after a telephone conversation this must be done by one of the individuals involved, so that both have an accurate record of what exactly has been agreed. In a committee meeting, in addition to the notes made by individuals, one person acts as the secretary and prepares minutes.

Personal memoranda – notes of your own thoughts, of ideas, of interpretations or questions that come to mind as other people speak – help you to ensure that otherwise fleeting thoughts are not forgotten. It is advisable to write your initials in the margin, next to each such note, as you write it – so that your own thoughts are not later confused with other people's contributions to any discussion.

Writing materials

A diary is useful for day-to-day records of such things as the times of appointments, organised classes and informal discussion groups. *Start every entry with the time.* Similarly, for work that necessitates the keeping of a detailed notebook (for example in field and laboratory investigations) *start every entry with the date and time.*

For all other notes use loose-leaf wide-lined A4 paper (210 × 297 mm). *Start every note with the date*, leave adequate margins and gaps between the lines for minor corrections and additions; and use only one side of each sheet – so that extra A4 sheets can be interleaved, if necessary, in appropriate places.

3   Discussing your work

In tutorials, seminars and discussion groups you have the opportunity: (a) to get to know other people (academic staff as well as students) whose interests are similar to your own; (b) to become accustomed to using the special vocabulary of your subject; (c) to benefit from the knowledge and experience of others; and (d) to develop personal skills needed for success as a student and in any career based on your studies.

Most people, although they find it easy to converse with friends, feel apprehensive when they have to speak in a seminar, discussion group or presentation; perhaps because they feel for the first time that they are addressing an audience.

Asking questions

The easiest way to get used to speaking in public is to ask questions, because you have time before asking a question to think about what exactly you need to know, and then when ready to ask the question you can say exactly what you have planned and this will not take long.

During the first meeting in any course of study, if this information has not already been provided in the course guide or in a separate handout, you should be given a list of lecture titles or of the topics you will be studying each week, with the lecturers' names and perhaps with suggestions for preliminary reading. Take the opportunity to ask any questions you have about the course. If you have any questions later, make a note so that you will remember either to find the answers yourself from other sources or to ask them, as appropriate, at the end of a lecture, in a practical class, or during a discussion on the subject in a seminar.

Asking questions in lectures and seminars

When listening during a lecture or seminar, as you make notes, write a question mark in the left-hand margin to signpost anything you write that you do not fully understand. Then you will be prepared, if there is time for questions or discussion during or at the end of the class, to ask for clarification or for further explanation. You are unlikely to be the only one who did not understand or would like to know more. Your questions will therefore help others as well as yourself, and will encourage others to ask questions – and everyone should learn from the lecturer's replies.

A lecture in which no questions are asked is much less rewarding for all concerned than one in which the students take a lively interest in the lecturer's words and in any handouts or visual aids. Good questions asked by those students who are taking an active interest help others to maintain their attention – to the questions, to the lecturer's replies, and to any discussion. They stimulate further thought. They help students to learn.

If you find a lecture uninteresting ask yourself: Did I prepare properly for this class? Was there anything I could not understand? Did I ask for further explanation? Was there no mention of a topic that I had expected to be included? Did I ask why it had not been considered? Did I ask for more information on any point? Would the lecture have been more interesting for other students if they too had asked questions that were in their minds? If students find a lecture on their subject uninteresting, what can they do to make it more interesting?

By indicating their interest, students make the work of lecturers more interesting and more rewarding. Questions in class should also be an important source of feedback for lecturers, helping them (a) to appreciate which aspects of the subject their students are finding difficult; and (b) to improve their lectures and make them more interesting.

Preparing for your next class

Rewriting your notes after a class simply to make them neater is a waste of time, but it is important to check them soon after each class: (a) to ensure you can understand them and that they include all the key points that you need to record; (b) to integrate them with other related notes; and (c) so that you can recognise topics on which you need further information. As you reflect on your work, you should note any questions that come to mind. If you are aware of the learning outcomes expected to be achieved in the class, you can also consider whether or not they were achieved. Then you can try to find the answers to your questions in your textbooks or from other sources before your next lecture in the series.

Your success in finding answers to your own questions will help you to gain confidence as a student, and will provide the basic understanding needed for further progress. You will be encouraged by your own efforts to further effective study. However, there will be times when you do not find the information you need. You may come across contradictions and not know whom to believe. You will then be ready to ask more good questions.

Most lecturers encourage questions and discussion during or at the end of each class, because no lecturer has time to ask every student, individually, 'How are you finding the work?' or 'Do you have any problems?' It is up to you to take the initiative and to ask questions if you need help – preferably in class so that other students can benefit from hearing both your question and the lecturer's reply.

Otherwise, if you choose an appropriate place and time, most lecturers will welcome your interest in their subject. You should therefore get to know the special interests of all your lecturers so that when you have a problem you will know whom to consult. Go prepared, with your questions and your notes, so that you can pinpoint your difficulty and get help quickly.

Getting the most out of group work

Conversations and discussions provide opportunities to develop your communication skills. Contributing to discussions will help you to gain confidence in speaking about your subject and to develop your ability: (a) to make your meaning clear; (b) to argue logically and tactfully; (c) to listen without interruption; (d) to consider different points of view and different explanations; (e) to observe the reactions of others to what is said; (f) to ask searching questions; (g) to disagree without causing offence; and (h) to express opinions and state the evidence upon which they are based.

In short, as you learn to participate effectively in discussions, you develop your ability to think and to express your thoughts. From the contributions of others you are able to correct misconceptions and misunderstandings, and may see things in a new light. And by organising your own thoughts, expressing them clearly, and answering questions, you will achieve a deeper understanding of your subjects (as teachers find when they start to teach any subject).

At the same time, as you listen to what others say and observe their non-verbal signals, you develop other interpersonal skills: paying attention to what people say, trying to appreciate their feelings and to see things from their different points of view, and adjusting your own contributions accordingly.

Tutorials

Until recently tutorials in which students received individual tuition from a tutor, by themselves or perhaps with one or two other students, were considered essential as part of a university education. Now, face-to-face tutorials are arranged mainly to provide students with the opportunity to discuss with a tutor any personal problem that is affecting their studies. Topics that used to be discussed in tutorials may now be discussed in interactive lectures or in tutor-led seminars, or may provide the basis for online activities.

The tutor organising an online activity writes: (a) a message comprising, for example, a problem which may be stated as a question; (b) an invitation to students to respond to the message; and (c) instructions on how to participate in the discussion (for examples, see Salmon, 2002). Students need only access to the Internet and a discussion board to which they can contribute, wherever they are (so courses can be global) and at any time (in so-called asynchronous working).

As well as contributing, by adding information or comments and by asking or answering questions, participants in an online discussion benefit from reading the contributions of others. They have time to reflect, and to use other sources of information, before and after each contribution. The tutor also looks at the discussion board regularly to offer advice, to help the discussion along if necessary, and to summarise at appropriate points.

As tutorials in which individual tuition is provided by a tutor have become less common in higher education more time has been allocated to seminars. These, like tutorials, are organised by a tutor and are usually concerned with aspects of the course content and the achievement of clearly stated course objectives or learning outcomes. Students benefit from experience in face-to-face discussions, as in a tutorial. That is to say, they are an aid both to learning and to the development of interpersonal skills.

Seminars

The course tutor will probably make clear the reason for including seminars as part of your course, list the topics to be discussed, provide guidance as to what is expected of students, and list the facilities available. Alternatively, this information may be included in written notes for guidance in the course handbook.

A large class of students will be organised in smaller groups for seminars. Four people are enough for a good discussion, and if more than six are present it may not be possible for everyone to make useful contributions in the limited time available (usually about fifty minutes). The best seating plan is one in which the participants sit in a circle facing one another,

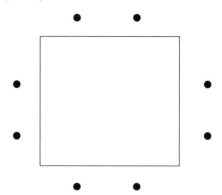

Figure 3.1   Seating arrangements for a seminar or small discussion group meeting, at which people sit upright, in a circle to facilitate eye contact, and preferably around a table so that everyone has space for note-making and for other papers.

and around a table so that everyone can sit upright and make notes (see Figure 3.1). With more than twelve students less suitable seating arrangements are unavoidable and the seminar is likely to be a question and answer session or a briefing rather than a discussion.

Tutor-led seminars

To start a seminar, the tutor will probably introduce the topic to be discussed. Then the discussion should involve all the students – with the tutor observing and speaking only when an intervention is necessary in open discussion.

However, early in a course when some students may have had no previous experience of working in groups, the tutor may, for example, need to encourage everyone to participate, ensure that no one speaks for too long, and try to ensure that important topics are not ignored.

In any seminar the tutor may ask questions at appropriate points to help the discussion along and to encourage critical thinking; and towards the end may, for example, correct any misunderstandings revealed in the discussion, try to summarise the main points raised, come to some conclusion, suggest sources of further information, or end with a few words of encouragement. If any criticism is constructive and tactfully expressed, it should be appreciated as necessary helpful advice from which all participants may benefit.

Before a seminar, given the title for the discussion, think about the subject and prepare a topic outline as you would when planning an essay

Table 3.1 Preparing for, and participating in, a discussion

Stages in preparation	Activities
Think	List relevant points.
	Prepare your first draft of a topic outline.
Plan	Note difficulties encountered, gaps in your knowledge, and questions.
	Consult your own notes and references cited in lectures.
	Try to find any further information you need, answer any questions, or solve any problems.
Write	Revise your topic outline.
	Number the points you consider should be made in the discussion, remembering that you need not make them all yourself.
	Note evidence or an example after each main point.
	List questions you could ask, remembering that some may be asked (or answers provided) by other participants.
	If you are to lead the discussion, try to anticipate questions that others might ask, and prepare a list of sources of further information.
	Listen to the discussion.
	Contribute. State your opinions and evidence. Explain. Ask questions. Make notes.
Revise	After the discussion review your lecture notes on the subject. Revise them if necessary. Reflect on your contributions to the discussion. What went well? How could you develop further your interpersonal skills?

(see Table 3.1). Look at the syllabus or the list of learning outcomes for the course so that you can see how the seminar fits in to the course as a whole. Look at your lecture notes on related topics and at other sources of information. Leave plenty of space in your topic outline so that you have space for additional notes as further relevant points come to mind during the discussion or are suggested by other participants.

Arrive at each seminar well prepared, with your topic outline, concise notes on each of the topics you consider relevant and likely to be included in the discussion, and a list of questions you would like to ask. Make sure that you have notepaper and any relevant lecture notes, so that you can make notes during the discussion, try to clear up any difficulties, or seek advice (for example, about further sources of information on particular points).

Take an active part in the discussion. Listen carefully. Be responsive: show your interest by your facial expressions and by concise interjections (see Table 2.1). Ask for clarification (When? Where? How can that be? Do you mean . . . ?). Ask other questions (see Table 2.2). Make each of your contributions short and to the point (see Table 3.2). If you use tutorials and other discussion groups in this way, you will learn both from your preparations and from the discussion.

Student-led seminars

Instead of the tutor, a student may be asked to introduce the topic that is to be discussed in a seminar, and perhaps also to lead the discussion. However, everyone present should have had the opportunity to consider the topic (as for a tutor-led seminar) and should arrive well prepared and ready to participate. The basis for a confident and successful performance when introducing and leading a seminar, as for a useful contribution by any other participant, is adequate preparation.

Before the seminar, if you have been asked to introduce the discussion, prepare a list of relevant topics that you consider should be discussed. Then decide which of these you should mention in your introduction. You may be able to mention the others when you contribute later in the discussion.

Many inexperienced speakers, when asked to introduce a discussion or to give a presentation, try to make too many points and to support each point with too much detail. Bear this in mind and, unless you are asked to do otherwise, complete your introduction in about one-fifth of the time available for the seminar. There will then be enough time for everyone present to take an active part in the discussion.

In a ten-minute introduction spend about two minutes on each of three or four of the topics listed in your plan. Emphasise why each one merits special attention in this seminar. Maintain eye contact to make sure everyone is listening. Speak loud enough for everyone to hear. Enunciate each word carefully: this may result in your speaking a little more slowly than you normally do in conversation.

If you have not introduced a seminar previously, you will find it helpful to rehearse what you intend to say, speaking aloud and making eye contact with your own image in a mirror each time you pause. By doing this you will learn, before the seminar, how little can be said, at an appropriate pace, with enough explanation, in the time available. If instead you ask one or two friends to listen to your rehearsal you will receive useful feedback that should help you, if necessary, to revise your plans and to improve your performance.

In the discussion, all contributions (comments, questions and answers) should be brief and to the point, including your own further contributions. As well as answering questions, you may mention other topics from your plan which you deliberately omitted from your introduction. You may find your notes on these topics helpful, for instance if you need to give more detail or to provide an example in response to someone else's contribution, or if you want to keep the discussion going when time is available and others are slow to contribute their views.

If in addition to introducing the subject you are also controlling the discussion, you must ensure that everyone who wishes to contribute has the opportunity to do so. As with a tutorial, a seminar is an opportunity for all present to learn by participating in the discussion (see Table 3.2), listening to other contributors, and making concise notes of points made in the discussion and of other points that could be made.

Table 3.2 Speaking to some purpose in a discussion

Agreeing
    That's right, . . .

Balancing
    On the one hand . . . , but

Disagreeing
    I don't follow your argument, wouldn't that mean . . .
    That's interesting, but have you considered . . .
    Another way of looking at things would be to . . .

Explaining
    Let me explain why . . .
    This is how it works . . .

Informing
    The problem is . . .
    We have been investigating . . .
    This is what happened . . .

Interpreting
    In other words, . . .

Questioning
    Am I right in thinking that . . .
    How do you account for . . .

Reinforcing
    The point is . . .

Reminding
    We must not forget . . .

Supporting
    I had a similar experience when . . .

As you try to explain things in a discussion, and as you listen to different interpretations of evidence, you think about the subject and reorganise your thoughts. By looking at the other participants you observe how everyone is responding to what is being said, in a way that is not possible when you are a member of an audience intent on listening to one person speak, as in a lecture.

If you are required to read a paper instead of speaking from notes, take care to speak more slowly than you would in normal conversation. Pause at appropriate points for emphasis (see page 60). Pause each time you move from one topic to the next; and take the opportunity to make eye contact with each of the other participants.

If you are not used to reading aloud or to reading in public, you will need to rehearse (as you would before speaking from notes, see page 30). The rehearsal will enable you to check that you are not trying to say too much in the time available (probably about ten minutes) or speaking too fast. Remember that you can read aloud much faster than you would normally speak in conversation, and that in a seminar people need time to understand and consider the thoughts you are trying to convey, and time to make notes.

After a tutorial or seminar, as after a lecture, it is helpful to reflect on the experience. Consider what you have learned; and amend your lecture notes so that all your notes on each topic are in one place. Integrating information from different sources, and going over things in your mind as you reconsider different aspects of your work, will also help you to remember important points.

The discussion in a seminar should be interesting and stimulating, but even in a student-led seminar much depends on the tutor's experience and personality. If the tutor dominates the proceedings, the seminar can too easily become a lecture. Even if the tutor says very little, the students are aware of the presence of someone who will at some time assess their work. Being anxious to appear in a favourable light, some may speak too much in an attempt to impress and some may be reluctant to speak in case they say the wrong things. Similarly, knowing that the student introducing a seminar is anxious to impress, other students may be inhibited in the discussion by not wishing to make things difficult for a friend.

Such considerations apply in all conversations; and one reason for organising discussions as part of higher education (see page 1) is to give students the opportunity to develop and practise the communication skills and other interpersonal skills needed in social life and in any profession.

Self-help groups

Talking over a difficult point after a class or after a period of private study, especially with someone who understands it better than you do, will help you with your work. Furthermore, you will benefit from explaining things to others – just as teachers find that they learn more by teaching a subject than they did, as students, from being taught. This is why when students are paired for peer-assisted learning (for example, when a good second year student is asked to help a first year student), both find that they benefit from the experience.

Because conversation and discussion are aids to thinking, understanding, learning and remembering, you may find it helpful to organise or join a self-help group (a peer-group of students with interests similar to your own) so that you can benefit from regular group study – as in a seminar but without a tutor (see Table 3.3).

First, the objectives of the group, to be pursued at each meeting and between meetings, should be agreed in relation to the course content, the learning outcomes expected, and the methods to be used in assessing their performance, as explained in the course handbook. Then each meeting must have a definite purpose, agreed at the previous meeting, so that all can arrive well prepared. In some tutorials you may have the opportunity to

Table 3.3 How conversation and discussion contribute to learning and to the acquisition and development of key personal skills

Key skills	Activities contributing to learning and personal development
Communicating	Formulating and expressing one's thoughts. Maintaining attention: listening, observing and interpreting verbal and non-verbal cues to the emotions and thoughts of others.
Finding information	Preparing for a discussion. Searching for relevant printed sources. Benefiting during and after discussions from the contributions of others.
Processing information	Assessing the value of information from different sources. Integrating material from different sources. Reviewing. Summarising.
Thinking critically	Considering contributions of others. Questioning. Reasoning from evidence. Explaining.
Team working	Preparing for discussion. Contributing to discussion. Agreeing and accepting responsibilities in group. Taking turns in leading discussions.
Time and stress management	Prioritising tasks. Working to job list. Completing tasks on time. Increasing self-confidence by being in control. Avoiding stress.

discuss an assignment with a tutor after it has been assessed. Similarly, in a self-help group you could discuss a tutor's comments written on your assignments and consider how you can benefit from any advice, or you could discuss some other previously agreed topic (for example, work done in preparation for a seminar, so that all present at the seminar will be better prepared).

Discussing a topic with other students can help to fix the main points in your mind as part of *revision*, and different ideas expressed may help you to see things in a new light. That is to say, taking part in a discussion is a stimulus to *thinking*. It can also add interest to your studies by providing a change from private study. It can provide *encouragement* by helping you to understand difficult points.

Participants in a discussion should approach it with an open mind. Having prepared, they should arrive at each meeting on time, with ideas they would like to share, prepared to consider different points of view and to benefit from the experience. Then, a serious discussion – as in a seminar – works best if the participants sit at a table, facing one another, with space for note-making (see Figure 3.1). As in a seminar, four is a good number for open discussion; and with more than six people some may find it difficult to take an active part.

In the discussion you will probably address one another by your first names but you should also get to know everyone's surname. Otherwise, after knowing them for some time you could find yourself in the position of being unable to introduce them to other people or, if you needed to contact them, unable to look up their names in a telephone directory. Most name badges are too small to be read by people who are far enough apart for comfortable conversation; so names are best displayed on a white card, folded like a tent, with the first name and surname written with a marker pen in large black letters that everybody can read as they sit at the table. These cards may be especially useful at the first few meetings, when people are getting to know one another (but it is good practice to display them at all committee meetings).

Arrive at group meetings well prepared, as you would for a seminar, but do not attempt to say all that you might like to say at once. *Speak clearly and concisely* each time you make a point. You will be surprised to find how much can be said in one minute; and two minutes with one person talking would begin to sound more like a lecture than a contribution to a discussion. *Listen carefully*, therefore, and *time your remarks* so that you speak only when you have something immediately relevant to say. For example, in discussing a problem you might speak early, add ideas from time to time, argue for or against particular approaches, and suggest a possible solution.

It helps when working in a peer-group, as in a committee, if someone agrees to lead the discussion (perhaps a different person for each meeting so that each student gains experience of this role). The leader can: (a) arrive early and ensure that each group member is met with a friendly greeting; (b) ensure that everyone's name is prominently displayed; (c) start the discussion on time; (d) remind participants of the purpose of the meeting (the topic or problem to be discussed); (e) encourage contributions from all those present; (f) discourage individuals who talk too often or for too long; (g) ensure that all contributions are relevant; and (h) towards the end of the meeting try to summarise the main points raised, state any conclusion agreed or decision made – including the choice of topic for discussion at the next self-help group meeting. If necessary, separate tasks should be allocated to members of the group – to be completed before the next meeting. See also *Leading a discussion*, page 106.

Self-help group meetings can be particularly useful for those studying part-time or mainly by correspondence course, or using other distance learning materials, who otherwise would have little face-to-face contact with people who share their interest in study. For such people, e-mail can provide a convenient means of contact with a tutor; and discussion boards enable students to leave messages and receive comments and advice – from other students or from the tutor.

Members of a peer-group that meets regularly may come to think of themselves as a team and benefit from team work in many ways that they could not have foreseen and that will differ from group to group. They may agree to work together in the first place because of their course of study, to facilitate their learning and for mutual support, but by getting to know one another better and sharing personal problems, as well as study problems, they may become life-long friends.

Team work

Any group of people with a common purpose, co-operating for their mutual benefit or to benefit the organisation to which they belong, may be called a team. Each team comprises: (a) a team leader, who may be involved in establishing the team and deciding its objectives, and in team selection; and (b) team members chosen to complement and support one another in achieving these objectives.

The success of a team depends on its including the right people (with the necessary balance of knowledge, experience and skills) and on their willing co-operation. At the outset everyone must consider the objectives and the time-scale set for their achievement. The team leader is then responsible: (a) for setting an example, in attitude and in well-directed effort; (b) for allocating tasks, listening and encouraging; (c) for monitoring progress; (d) for arranging meetings and, when chairing a meeting, for keeping to the agenda, encouraging contributions, and ensuring each contribution is concise and to the point; and (e) for ensuring that the work is completed on time.

Arguing a case

In any conversation or discussion you may need to convince others of the correctness of a conclusion or to persuade them of the appropriateness of a particular course of action. In this context, to argue is not necessarily to disagree with anyone. It is simply to provide evidence or to give good and sufficient reasons for the views you express.

In arguing, you can begin with particular instances or observations (examples), which you may state as facts, leading to your conclusion (which may be a generalisation). This is *inductive reasoning*. Each example must include enough detail of a particular relevant object or event.

Alternatively, you can begin with a generalisation (a premise) and apply it so as to draw a conclusion regarding a particular case. This is *deductive reasoning*. A *premise* is an introductory statement or proposition – affirming or denying something – as a basis for argument (for example, 'All men are equal'); and *logical argument* based on a true premise should lead to a valid conclusion.

An analogy, in which one thing is compared with another, can help a speaker to make a point. It might be said, for example, that a talk or presentation is like an old-fashioned railway train, with an engine, a number of carriages, and a guards van: the parts are linked but each one serves a different purpose (introduction – topic 1 – topic 2 – topic 3 – conclusion).

When trying to persuade people to agree to your suggestion, to adopt a particular policy, or to come to what you consider to be the right conclusion, in presenting evidence in support of the decision you favour you must also be aware of the evidence against. Then in presenting your case you may be able to counter the arguments of those who seem not yet convinced. Or you may say briefly why you do not support one conclusion and why you do support another (providing a contrast, see *Be persuasive*, page 40).

Errors in an argument, whether or not these are deliberate, may be the result of making incorrect statements (telling an untrue story) or of omitting relevant information (not telling the whole story). It is difficult and perhaps impossible to avoid either of these sources of error, because we know few things with certainty and so can rarely know the whole truth.

Intelligent people are most likely to be convinced by evidence that is presented clearly, forcefully and persuasively. And, where possible, it is important to be precise.

Be forceful

You are most likely to make friends and influence people (obtaining their willing co-operation) if you are *assertive* (well mannered, self-confident, expressing your views clearly and if necessary forcefully, but pleased to collaborate and willing to consider seriously the views of others), rather than *submissive* (appearing to lack confidence, reluctant to express an opinion or to voice opposition when necessary) or *aggressive* (arrogant, autocratic, blunt, dogmatic, inconsiderate, inclined to blame others when things go wrong).

The use of forceful language depends on adequate preparation, so that you can use carefully chosen words (see chapter 4 *Choosing the right word*) in well-constructed sentences (see chapter 5 *Using words effectively*) to provide persuasive evidence in an appropriate order, and arrive at compelling conclusions.

In speaking forcefully you could further emphasise each step in an argument by your intonation, by your facial expressions, by appropriate gestures, and by meaningful pauses.

> *Prefer the active to the passive voice.* Instead of 'It should be remembered that', say 'Remember' (see Table 5.6).
>
> *Prefer concrete nouns* (the names of things you can touch and see) *to abstract nouns* (see Table 5.5).
>
> *Prefer the positive to the negative.* When coaching rugby football, instead of saying 'Do not carry the ball across the field', say 'Head for the try line'.

'Ask not what America can do for you, ask what *you* can do for America': note how the word *not* in the first of these two statements in antithesis can add force to the second positive statement, as can the repetition of an important word in the second:

> *Prefer the specific to the general.* An example is easier to remember than are all the steps in an argument leading to a conclusion or a summary of all the evidence leading to a generalisation.

For maximum impact, start most contributions with the point you wish to emphasise (as with the topic for most paragraphs). Then keep to the point (see *Emphasise the most important points*, page 60).

Be persuasive

People are most likely to be persuaded (Napley, 1975) if, in addition to being convincing (enthusiastic and providing evidence to support your argument), you are *brief* (speak for no longer than is necessary), *concise* (use no more words than are necessary) and *sincere* (as judged by eye contact, by facial expression and by your reputation), with no trace of pomposity, and if what you say is *interesting* (*relevant* to the needs of your audience, in an appropriate *order*, and with enough *explanation* to ensure everyone understands).

Antitheses (two thoughts placed in opposition) can be very effective in presenting two sides of an argument concisely (for example, in making a distinction between wrong and right, or positioning them versus us). For example, a politician might say: 'Some people think . . . , *but* I say that . . .', implying that the first statement is false and saying that the second is true; or when attempting to make an audience identify with a cause, might say: 'They tell us that . . . , but we know that . . .'. Such statements have the advantage of brevity and, if well chosen and clearly expressed, may be a complete and memorable message. For example: 'Man is born free and everywhere is in chains' (Jean-Jacques Rousseau, *The Social Contract*, 1762), and 'All animals are equal, but some are more equal than others' (George Orwell, *Animal Farm*, 1945).

When trying to persuade people whether to consider, to listen, to do, or to buy, their opposition could be due, for example, (a) to resistance to change; or (b) to fears related to self-interest. You must be clear in your own mind, therefore, as to what you are trying to achieve.

On the one hand, if arguing in favour of a proposed change you would speak of the reasons for change. On the other hand, if opposing the change you would point out why the change is undesirable.

Whatever you are trying to persuade people to do or to think, they may expect you to show an awareness of differences of opinion or of possible courses of action but you must leave no doubt as to your own preference. And you must anticipate questions and possible objections so that you are prepared to answer questions or to offer further explanation if necessary.

The techniques of persuasion as used in advertising, to play on our needs (for food, shelter, warmth and security) and on our fantasies and desires (for success, prestige, power), are outside the scope of this book. So is propaganda, in which those attempting to gain acceptance of their opinions or beliefs use techniques of persuasion, especially repetition, in attempts to conceal rather than to tell the truth. But we should be persuasive, when appropriate, not to assert that what is wrong is right but to convince others as to the truth of what is right.

Quiller-Couch (1906), in *From a Cornish Window*, asks:

> What forbids a man, who has the truth to tell, from putting it as persuasively as possible? . . . Will you only commend persuasiveness in a sophist who engages to make the worst argument appear better, and condemn it in a teacher who employs it to enforce truth?

Be precise

Prefer the definite to the vague. A politician may use vague words to express hopes when it is not possible to be precise: saying, for example, that a fund will be established of *substantial* size and *adequate* coverage over a *considerable* period. But be precise if you can. Avoid words that draw attention to vague statements (for example, *few, many, heavy, long, thin, slow, soon*).

> 'Whenever anyone says I can do something soon I'll say to them yes, I know all about that . . . , but when, when, when?'
> *Key to the Door*, Alan Sillitoe (1961)

Be precise when you can. Instead of saying *for a decade*, say *for ten years*; instead of *for about a decade*, say for how long; instead of *for almost a quarter of a century*, say for how many years.

Use numbers so that you can say how many, and use numbers with International System units of measurement (see *Standards*, page 115) so that you can say, for example, how much, how heavy, how long, how thick, how fast. Instead of saying soon, say when.

Consider the meaning you wish to convey before using the word *very* with an adverb (*very quickly*) or with an adjective (*very large*), and before using adverbs (for example, *slowly*) or adjectives (for example, *appreciable, cheap, enough, heavy, large, typical* and *small*) or modifying and intensifying words (for example, *comparatively, exceptionally, extremely, fairly, quite, rather, really, relatively, sufficiently* and *unduly*). Such modifiers indicate only that you are either unable or unwilling to be precise. If you use them in an attempt to make an argument more convincing they will probably have the opposite effect – making it less clear and less persuasive.

Disagreeing without causing offence

Usually, it is best to avoid outright disagreement. Remember the song 'Two Lovely Black Eyes', written by Charles Coburn in 1886 for the old English music hall:

> Two lovely black eyes!
> Oh! what a surprise!
> Only for telling a man he was wrong,
> Two lovely black eyes!

Rather than reacting at once with 'I disagree', you might provide an alternative interpretation of evidence leading to a different conclusion: 'I accept most of what you say, but . . . ' or 'I am not convinced that we should, because . . . ' . Or you might say 'That's interesting' or 'That's a good point', which would not prevent you, later in the discussion, from supporting a different course of action or from expressing a different point of view, saying: 'Another possibility is . . . ' or 'I suggest we consider . . . ' or 'Wouldn't it be better if we . . . '.

Another way to avoid outright disagreement is to ask a question, to see if a speaker is able to provide any further explanation or add evidence in support of an opinion or conclusion different from your own, for example: 'Why is that?' or 'How would that work?' or 'How do you reconcile that with the observation that . . . ?' or 'What do you think about . . . ?' or 'What do you consider the advantages and disadvantages of that procedure?'

To begin by saying 'With respect . . . ' is merely to send a warning signal that you are about to disagree. It does not soften the blow! It is better to be positive: 'I can see that, and . . . ', 'That's true, but look at it this way . . . ', 'A similar thing happened to me, but . . . '.

If you needed to give the matter further thought, you might say: 'I am not sure, I need time to consider the possibilities' or 'I can't comment now, I'll need to consult . . . '. Your response to adverse criticism might be: 'What exactly is the problem?' When responding to untruths you might say: 'That's not right; what happened was . . . '. Or if you accepted that you had made a mistake you might say: 'Sorry about that; I am now . . . '.

When students participate in a seminar or meet as a self-help group, the pervading atmosphere should be one of serious discussion and friendly co-operation. There is a need for tolerance, for an openness to suggestions, and as in normal conversation for mutual respect (see *Be polite*, page 7). Free discussion, with the exchange of ideas, is inhibited unless dissent based on reasoned argument is welcomed in any discussion involving responsible, self-confident individuals.

Improve your performance

Assessing your performance

After a tutorial, seminar or other group work, it is important to review your notes and to reflect on your own performance – as you would after completing any practical work or any written assignment. What have you learned from the discussion that has contributed to your understanding of your subject? Has your participation contributed to the development of your interpersonal skills? Keep a written record (a reflective log) of this critical assessment: of things you did well, of things you could do better, and of mistakes you do not intend to repeat. Doing this as a matter of routine will help you, as a mature learner, to benefit from your own experience as well as from the advice and comments of others, as you accept more and more responsibility for your own learning and continue to develop the personal skills needed for success as a student and in any career based on your studies.

Assessing students' performance in seminars and in other group work

Students should be motivated in their attempts to improve their communication skills, as in other aspects of personal development, (a) by their recognition of the importance of these skills in contributing to their success as students and in any career based on their studies; and (b) by the improvements they see in their own performance as a result of the advice, guidance and training provided as part of the course. It should not be necessary to assess the performance of students simply to make them take group work seriously.

However, if you find that you are to be assessed on your performance in seminars, or if you are part of a team that is to be assessed as a group, you will need to know what is to be assessed (for example, organisation of material, content, delivery, quality and use of visual aids; answers to questions and, if appropriate, contributions to the discussion or discussion leading; and team work) and you should be told how these different aspects will be assessed.

All concerned (both academic staff and students) *must* be given proper training and adequate practice so that they can develop the necessary skills *before* they either assess others or are assessed themselves.

To assess students while they were still learning how to improve their performance, and before they had completed the course intended to help them to develop and practise the necessary skills, *would be contrary to the whole spirit of education*, in that an attempt would be being made to assess a desired outcome of the course before it was possible to know the outcome.

For the same reason, any observation of the performance of students in seminars and presentations intended to promote the students' learning (their knowledge and understanding of their subject) *should* be made: (a) to provide constructive feedback, so that the class as a whole, as well as individual students, can be instructed, advised and guided; and (b) so that improvements noted during the course can be used in assessing the success of the methods of instruction used, and the advice and guidance provided, as part of the course.

That is to say, the continuous assessment of coursework (in class exercises, tests and homework) should be used only in attempts either to improve student performance by providing practice and feedback (in so-called formative assessment) or, when assessing the course, to improve it. Students who improve their performance throughout a course *should not* be down-graded, when grades for a subject are decided at the end of a course of study, because at some time earlier in the course, when still learning and developing their oral communication skills, they were unable to perform as well as they did at the end. That is to say, the grades awarded at the end of a course *should* reflect the knowledge and ability of the students when they have had the opportunity to benefit from the course (as judged by so-called summative assessment).

Group work, in which students divide responsibilities and share ideas and data, involves much more than the development of oral communication skills. The problems involved in attempting a fair assessment of the performance of individual members of such a group, and of the group as a whole, are outside the scope of this book. However, it is important to distinguish between collaboration, which is involved in all successful group work and team work, and collusion. Having co-operated in group work you must evaluate the information you have obtained from different sources, decide what to include and how best to arrange your material, and prepare by yourself *any work you submit for assessment as your own work*: making clear your knowledge of the subject, your interpretation of evidence, your reasoning, your understanding and your conclusions. Collusion, like fabrication and plagiarism, is cheating and is always unacceptable.

Serving on a committee

The best way to improve your performance in any game is by participating, because you learn from those who already play well (and admire their prowess). So, if you belong to any student societies, take the opportunity to serve on a committee. This will give you experience of how the committee works, which will be useful when you serve on other committees related to your work or to your leisure interests, and you may meet people studying different subjects whose academic interests differ from your own.

You may also have opportunities to be a student representative on an academic committee in your college or university, or to serve on a committee unconnected with your studies, in the local community. Active membership of any committee is a useful practical training for management; and you will make useful contacts with people from different walks of life whose interests are similar to your own. However, take care not to allow yourself to be persuaded to take on too much committee work – or tasks involving extra responsibility on any committee – unless you are sure that you can afford the time and that the extra work will not interfere adversely with your studies or your need for recreation.

Recording lines of communication

If in a seminar or other group discussion, whenever anyone is addressing someone directly, you draw a line on a diagram (similar to Figure 3.1, page 30) connecting the person speaking to the person being addressed, you will have a record of lines of communication (forming a *participation pattern*). You will probably find that each person is more likely to speak to the people with whom they have eye contact than to those sitting at their sides. Consider this when you are deciding where to sit.

Note also that when a tutor is present, the lines of communication are likely to be between student and tutor rather than student and student. This is something a tutor should be aware of, so that open discussion between students can be encouraged.

Video conferencing

Many colleges and universities use video conference facilities so that, for example, people in other locations can participate in their seminars (as in many television news programmes when a presenter in the studio converses with a reporter in another country).

Before a video conference each contributor must know what subject is to be discussed, and have adequate time for preparation. Before agreeing to participate, you will also need to know the aspect of the subject upon which you may be expected to contribute. Given this information, it is helpful to prepare as you would for a tutorial or seminar (see page 30) and to have notes to which you can refer, even though when speaking you will look at the camera (at the person you are addressing) for most of the time.

Because participants are in different locations, it helps if those planning the discussion (including the positioning and use of cameras and microphones) have considered what questions are likely to be asked – and, where possible, have been given notice of some of the points participants would like to make. As for any meeting, the discussion leader must decide before the discussion starts: (a) what is to be achieved in the time available (the purpose of the seminar); (b) what information is needed before decisions can be taken or conclusions reached (the agenda); and (c) what questions to ask to ensure that this information is obtained and the seminar brought to a satisfactory close (with decisions made or conclusions reached).

As in a television interview, when speaking you can be seen by everyone who is watching the screen (by all those participating in the seminar) but how much they see of you, and how much background, will depend on the decisions of people directing or operating your camera. Viewers may see just your face, and respond to your eye movements and facial expressions as well as to your voice; or they may also see your dress and posture – and movements of your shoulders, arms and hands that convey additional information about your feelings. In the background, which should help to create an appropriate atmosphere for the seminar and help viewers to understand each speaker's situation, there should be no distractions.

Similarly what you see as you respond to a question may be just the face of the questioner, as in a video phone call, but it helps – particularly at the start of a discussion – if you can see everyone who is to participate and how they are sitting. For a small group it is also important to know each person's name (displayed on a card on the table, or electronically on the screen both at the start and again as each person speaks).

Look at the camera, which is usually close to the monitor, when you speak. This eye contact is especially important at the beginning of a conversation, when viewers are forming their first impressions (see page 1). If your own image is displayed in a corner of the screen you will be able to confirm that you are looking at the camera.

If your contribution is directed to a particular person, say whom you are addressing so that this is clear to everyone involved. Assume that your microphone is working and that you can be heard. Try to speak as you would in normal conversation but be particularly careful to articulate each word clearly. You may need to pause for a couple of seconds after you have made a point (for slightly longer than you might in a face-to-face conversation) to give the person you are addressing time to hear your words and if necessary to respond, before you continue with your next point.

Because you must look at the camera most of the time, and some participants will be in other locations, you will be unable to see how everyone is reacting to your message. That is to say, you will not receive as much feedback as you would in a face-to-face conversation or discussion.

There will probably be a light on your microphone to indicate when it is live. However, whether or not it has a light, ensure that your microphone is muted when you are not speaking. Otherwise background noises (caused, for example, by people shuffling papers) will cause distracting interference with other speakers' contributions.

Preparing a poster presentation

Poster presentations are used at conferences, in exhibitions, and as part of displays on open days, to draw attention, for example, to recent developments, new equipment, and work in progress. The preparation of a poster is also a useful exercise for students: to encourage their development of good communication skills, and as a basis for a discussion on any subject.

When preparing a poster, consider what is needed to attract attention. Remember that a poster is a visual aid for use not when addressing a large audience but when speaking to individuals who come to look at the display one or two at a time, and to discuss your work. It should not include too much detail.

Normally at a conference, exhibition or open day people stand next to their posters, at times allocated in the programme, ready to discuss their work with anyone who expresses an interest. But, if appropriate, they also prepare a handout for those who require more detail than should be included on a poster; and leave copies in a pocket below the poster so that they are available when no one is present to answer questions.

Give your poster an eye-catching title. For the title, and for other words that you want people to see at a distance, use large letters (and a sans serif font, for example **ARIAL**). Indicate sequences in your display by large numbers or by arrows. Place any diagrams or photographs together if they are to be compared; and ensure that anything requiring close examination is at eye level. Be brief: leave enough space between parts of the poster; resist the temptation to include more information than can be understood by non-specialists in a few minutes.

4   Choosing the right word

Use the right word

Simeon Potter in *Our Language* (1966) began by saying that we cannot know too much about the language we speak, even though most of us can get along without knowing very much about it: 'But knowledge is power. The power of rightly chosen words is very great, whether those words are intended to inform, to entertain, or to move.'

For many years the *Reader's Digest* magazine included a regular feature headed 'It pays to increase your word power'; and every day in newspapers there are crossword puzzles and other word games. Clearly, many people who do not think of themselves as students take an interest in words. There is fun to be had from words.

In speaking you put your thoughts into words as you try to tell others what you think. It follows, if you take an interest in words, that as you enlarge your vocabulary you improve your ability to think and to express your thoughts. Then clarity in speech depends on choosing the right words to convey your meaning, arranging them in well-constructed sentences, and pronouncing them distinctly.

In an unpublished essay on 'The Scaffolding of Rhetoric' (Churchill, 1897), Winston Churchill, later widely acknowledged as a great orator, wrote that 'Knowledge of a language is measured by the nice and exact appreciation of words'. He considered the most important element in rhetoric to be the continual employment of the best word: the one that expresses, absolutely, the full meaning of the speaker.

Some words that many people confuse

One of the delights of English is its rich vocabulary. Two words may be very similar in spelling and pronunciation but different in meaning, so that the choice of one when you should be using the other is likely to confuse those who don't notice your mistake and may amuse those who do.

When Mrs Malaprop in Sheridan's *The Rivals* (1775) says 'Sure, if I *reprehend* anything in the world, it is the use of my *oracular* tongue, and a nice *derangement* of *epitaphs*', her achievements in the confusion of words are incredible (Fowler, 1968); but the use of one word when another is clearly needed (for example, *apprehend*, *vernacular*, *arrangement* and *epithets* by Mrs Malaprop) is not uncommon in conversation (or even in writing – when there is more time for thought and for second thoughts).

When the wrong word is used, even if most people take the right meaning, the mistake distracts attention from the message and creates an unfavourable impression. To illustrate the need for care in the choice of words and in their pronunciation, so that it is clear which words are being used, consider the following pairs of words. They are similar in sound but very different in meaning; and many people confuse them – and so use one when they should be using the other. Concise comments are included, in parentheses, to make clear the differences in meaning.

Accept (receive) and *except* (not including).

Advice (suggestions) and *advise* (to give advice).

Alternate (to perform by turns), *alternately* (first one thing then an alternative, repeatedly, as with a light flashing on and off) and *alternatively* (referring to one thing as an alternative to another). Strictly, therefore, one thing may be an *alternative* to another but with more than two to choose from you have a *choice*, not alternatives.

Affect (to alter, influence, have an effect on) and *effect* (to bring about, or a result).

Beside (at the side of) and *besides* (as well as).

Complement (to add to or to make complete) and *compliment* (to congratulate, or an expression of regard). *Complementary* means *adding to*, and *complimentary* means *without charge*.

Continuous (non-stop) and *continual* (repeatedly).

Council (a committee) and *counsel* (advice, an adviser, or to advise).

Dependant (one who is dependent on another) and *dependent* (relying on).

Discreet (circumspect, prudent) and *discrete* (entire, separate).

Farther (more distant) and *further* (additional).

Forego (go before) and *forgo* (do without).

Fortuitous (accidental) and *fortunate* (lucky).

Homogenous (of similar consistency throughout) and *homogeneous* (of the same kind or nature).

Imply and *infer*: a speaker or writer may imply (hint at) more than is actually said or written, and from this the listener or reader may infer (guess or understand) the intended meaning.

Method (how to perform a task) and *methodology* (the study of method).

Parameter (a characteristic of a population, estimates of which are called statistics) and *perimeter* (a boundary).

Partially (biased) and *partly* (in part).

Practice (a noun) and *practise* (a verb).

Practicable (something that could be done) and *practical* (not theoretical). A project may be considered impracticable because it is not cost effective, but to say that something is not a practical proposition means that it could not be done.

Principal (first in rank, main, original or capital sum) and *principle* (a fundamental truth, a law of science, or a rule of conduct one is unlikely to break – as in a matter of principle).

While (at the same time as) and *whilst* (although).

Other words that many people misuse

The following words are misunderstood, and therefore misused, by many people.

Aggravate (make worse) is used by some people when they mean *annoy* (trouble or vex).

Amount refers to the mass or volume of something measured and should not be used for the *number* of things counted.

Anticipate (forestall, act before something happens) and *expect* (think that something will happen).

Approximate(ly) means very *close(ly)* and should not be used if *about* or *roughly* would be better.

To *argue* is to state reasons for an opinion or evidence in support of a conclusion, whereas to *disagree* is to be of a different opinion.

Data are facts of any kind, including both measurements recorded as numbers and other observations recorded as words. They should not be confused with *results* (obtained from data by deduction, calculation or data processing). It is incorrect, therefore, to speak of raw data, but correct to refer to original observations as original data.

Disinterested means *impartial*, whereas *uninterested* means *not interested*.

Fewer means a smaller number whereas *less* means a smaller mass or volume, so it is not possible, for example, to have less people.

Literally (meaning actually) should not be used in an attempt to affirm the truth of an exaggeration, as in 'His eyes were literally glued to the television screen'.

Logical, *sensible* and *appropriate* are not synonyms. An appropriate or sensible order of topics in a talk, as in a document, is not necessarily a logical order (see page 74).

Majority means the greater number, the excess of one number over another, whereas *most* means nearly all. In an election a majority is the number by which the votes for the winning candidate exceeds those for the candidate who comes second. If you read that 'the majority of writers use word processors', does this mean nearly all writers use them? Does anyone know what proportion of writers use them? Would it be better to say simply that many writers use them? What is the difference quantitatively between the majority and the vast majority? Clearly, some people use the word *majority* as a substitute for evidence – when they are unable to be precise.

The word *often* (frequently) is used by many people (see Table 4.1) when the word they need is *many* (numerous). People who eat wild mushrooms often die (but people who do not eat them die only once).

Oral means *spoken* and *verbal* means *using words*. In speaking face to face we use facial expressions and other body language (non-verbal communication) as well as words, whereas in conversations on the telephone (unless it is a video call) we use only words (in wholly verbal communication).

Progress means a move forward or a change from worse to better, but this word is misused deliberately by many people in attempts to persuade others to accept changes that are clearly not improvements.

The *range*, in statistics, is recorded as the largest and smallest of a sample, or the difference between these measurements.

Table 4.1 The word *often* misused

Don't say often	*If you mean* many
The houses were large in size and often inadequately heated.	The houses were large, and many were inadequately heated.
One reason why reports are often not well written is . . .	One reason many reports are badly written is . . .
People often may not know the meaning of words which seem obvious to you.	Many people may not understand words familiar to you.
When people see a word processor for the first time they are often amazed.	Many people are amazed when they see a word processor for the first time.

The word *refute* should be used in the sense of proving falsity or error, not as if it were a synonym for *deny*, *reject* or *repudiate*.

Significant is a statistical term with a precise meaning, so care is needed in using it in other contexts if readers are to know whether or not you mean *statistically significant*.

Statistics are numerical data systematically collected, and the results of the analysis of such data.

Viable means capable of independent life, whereas *feasible* means that something can be done.

The word *vital* means *essential to life* and should not be used for something that is *essential* in some other way.

Within (enclosed by) and *in* (inside) differ in meaning. Something may be within these walls or within the bounds of possibility, but unless some such limits are intended the word *in* should be preferred.

Other commonly misused words are: *admitted* (for *said*), *always* (for *everywhere*), *centre* (for *middle*), *centred around* (for *centred on*), *circle* (for *disc*), it *comprises of* (for it *comprises*, or it *consists of*), *degree* (for *extent*), *either* (for *each* or *both*), *except* (for *unless*), *generally* (for *usually*), *if* (for *although*), *importantly* (for *important*), *improvement* (for *alteration* or *change*), *lengthy* (for *long*), *limited* (for *few*, *small*, *slight* or *narrow*), *minor* (for *little*), *myself* (for *me*), *natural* (for *normal*), *optimistic* (for *hopeful*), *optimum* (for *highest*), *percentage* (for *some*), *same* (for *similar*), *since* (for *because*), *singular* or *unique* (for *rare* or *notable*), *sometimes* (referring to place instead of time), *superior* (for *better than*), *transpire* (for *happen*), *virtually* (for *almost*), *volume* (for *amount*), *weather* (for *climate*), and *wastage* (for *waste*). See also *Distinguish between facts and speculation* (page 23).

Keep it simple

Matthew Arnold considered that the secret of style in writing is to have something to say and to say it as simply as you can. Simplicity is even more important when speaking because, unless you repeat words for emphasis, listeners have only the one chance to comprehend your message. So, whether speaking or writing, it is always best to try to express your thoughts as clearly and simply as you can.

The words you choose to express your thoughts, like the thoughts you choose to express and the way you express them, will depend on your purpose, on your audience, and on the occasion. But always try to use words that convey your meaning precisely – and if in doubt refer to a dictionary to make sure you are using the right word.

Avoid grandiloquence

You may use words familiar to both yourself and your listeners, yet construct long sentences that are difficult to understand. And if you use too many long words, when shorter words would be more appropriate (see Table 4.2), your studied avoidance of simplicity is more likely to annoy, amuse or confuse than to impress.

This anonymous version of a well-known nursery rhyme pokes fun at grandiloquence:

> Scintillate, scintillate, globule aurific,
> Fain would I fathom thy nature specific,
> Loftily poised in the ether capacious,
> Strongly resembling a gem carbonaceous.

Churchill (1897) wrote:

> The shorter words of a language are usually more ancient. Their meaning is more ingrained in the national character and they appeal with greater force . . . than words recently introduced from the Latin and the Greek. [Prefer the] short, homely words of common usage – so long as such words can fully express [your] thoughts and feelings.

Similarly, the advice of Fowler and Fowler (1906), repeated by Quiller-Couch (1916), is to: 'Prefer the short word to the long. Prefer the Saxon word to the Romance.'

Always prefer the short word to the longer word if the short word will serve your purpose better. Also, for the sake of accuracy, as well as for

Table 4.2 Prefer a short word to a longer word unless the longer word will serve your purpose better

Instead of this	Prefer this	Instead of this	Prefer this
absolutely	yes	individuals	people
accordingly	so	inform	tell
adequate	enough	manufacture	make
application	use	partially	partly
approximately	about	peruse	read
acquaint	tell	presently	soon[b]
assistance	help	purchase	buy
concerning	about	regarding	about
consequently	so	request	ask
currently[a]	now	streamlined	shortened
demonstrate	show	subsequently	later[b]
despatch	send	sufficient	enough
encounter	meet	terminate	end
endeavour	try	upon	on
fabricate	build	utilisation	use
firstly	first	utilise	use
forward	send	virtually	almost
importantly	important	within	in

Notes
a   Should usually be omitted.
b   Be precise if you can; say when.

brevity, in any serious conversation, avoid hyperbole (exaggeration) – as in the use of words the words *awesome*, *fabulous* and *fantastic* in contexts that have nothing to do with awe, fable or fantasy.

Improve your performance

Use a dictionary

Do use your computer spelling checker when you have completed any word-processed document. However, remember that although a spelling checker may help you to spell a word correctly it will not confirm that it is the word needed to convey the meaning you intended. Using a spelling checker is not an alternative to using a dictionary.

Always have a good dictionary to hand on your bookshelf or in your desk drawer. Use it not only to check the spelling of a word but also to check its pronunciation, its function (for example, n. = noun, v. = verb), its current status in the language (standard, colloquial or slang), its derivation (origins), its derivatives (words formed from it) and its several meanings. If you take an interest in words you will find a dictionary that gives all this information a life-long source of enlightenment, interest and pleasure.

Choose words with care

1 Consider all the words listed in this chapter (pages 49–52) and in chapter 2 (page 23), which many people use incorrectly, to check that you know their meaning and can use them correctly.
2 Cover the words in column two of Table 4.2 and think of shorter words that would probably serve your purpose better in most contexts than those in column one. Then check your answers against those suggested in column two. Repeat this exercise with the words in column three, while those in column four are covered.

Avoid specialist terms

Many of the specialist terms used in your studies, which you understand and which make for easy communication between specialists, are not used by non-specialists and may not be understood by students whose special interests differ from your own. So it is best to avoid such terms, unless you are sure that everyone present will understand them.

If you must use a term that some of those present may not understand, you must first define it concisely using everyday words. If you do not help non-specialists to understand specialist terms, to which they may refer disparagingly as jargon, they will not be impressed and will probably lose interest in your message.

One way of providing a concise explanation is to add a summarising phrase (signposted, for example, by the words *That is*, or *That is to say*, or *In short*, or *In other words*) in which everyday words are used instead of the long words or specialist terms that may not be understood by some people. Such was the habit of Mr Micawber:

> 'Under the impression . . . that your peregrinations in this metropolis have not as yet been extensive, and that you might have some difficulty in penetrating the arcana of the Modern Babylon in the direction of the City Road – in short,' said Mr Micawber, in another burst of confidence, 'that you might lose yourself . . .'
>
> *David Copperfield*, Charles Dickens (1850)

Similarly, in Frank Loesser's lyric for the musical *Guys and Dolls*, written in 1953, Miss Adelaide reads in a technical publication that she has symptoms of a psychosomatic disorder affecting the upper respiratory tract and concludes that '*in other words*', she has a cough.

Avoid abbreviations, contractions and acronyms

Abbreviations are acceptable in writing because they can be explained in parenthesis when first used, or in a glossary, but they should not be used when speaking (or in the visual aids used to support a talk) unless, like the symbols for SI units of measurement, the initials W.H.O. and the acronym UNESCO, they are so well known to your audience as to require no explanation.

Avoid *abbreviations*, shortened forms of words, because each one may have several meanings (for example, adv. = advent, advocate, adverb, advertisement; d. = daughter, day, dead, dollar, dose, pence) and may not be understood by some people. This is also true of *contractions*, which include the first and last letters of a word (for example, Mr and Dr), and of *acronyms*, which comprise the initial letters of successive words and may be pronounced as if they were words (for example UNO, United Nations Organisation). Furthermore, abbreviations, contractions and acronyms in common use in one country may not be understood in another; and the abbreviations used by one person in a text message (txt msg) may not be understood by another even in the same family.

5   Using words effectively

Say what you mean

In a dictionary each word is first explained and then used in appropriate contexts to make its several meanings clear. This is necessary because words do not stand alone: each one gives meaning to and takes meaning from the sentence, so that there is more to the whole than might be expected from its parts.

The position of a word

William Cobbett (1736–1835) wrote of grammar as a science, concerned with choosing the words that ought to be employed and placing them where they ought to be placed:

> In order to obtain the co-operation, the concurrence, or the consent of others, we must communicate our thoughts to them. The means of communication are *words*; and grammar teaches us *how to make use of words*. Therefore, in all the . . . situations of life, a knowledge of the principles and rules of grammar must be useful; in some situations it must be necessary to the avoiding of really injurious errors . . .
>
> (Cobbett, 1819)

Jonathan Swift defined a good style as proper words in proper places. Where you place a word in a sentence may, for example, reflect the emphasis you wish to put upon it. An important word may come near the beginning or near the end; and in either position it may help to link the ideas expressed in successive sentences. But word order is always important, because if any words are misplaced the meaning of a sentence may not be the meaning intended.

Consider, for example, this expensive notice at a business entrance: 'Please do not obstruct access by parking opposite these gates'. This could be interpreted as a request to park opposite the gates, but the meaning intended is probably: 'Please do not park opposite these gates'.

The Member Panel co-ordinator who wrote 'As a valued member of the Society's Member Panel, I hope that you will . . . ' (meaning that the co-ordinator is the valued member) should have written 'I should be grateful if you, as a valued member of the Society's panel, would . . . '

A booklet on report writing included the claim: 'This booklet will help you to write serious and professional, but not necessarily dry, humourless reports.' Presumably, the authors did not intend the booklet to help people write humourless reports. Quite the opposite! They meant 'reports that are serious and professional but not necessarily dry and humourless'. Placing the word reports earlier in the sentence helps to emphasise the intention to *help you to write reports*. This would be especially important in a talk because listeners must grasp our meaning as we speak: 'This talk is to help you write reports that are serious and professional, but not necessarily dry and humourless.'

The word *only* is well known for the trouble it may cause when out of place. Consider, for example, the meaning of each of the following sentences.

Only we open from 0900–1200 h on Saturdays. (No one else does.)

We only open from 0900–1200 h on Saturdays. (All we do, from 0900 to 1200 h on Saturdays, is open.)

We open only from 0900–1200 h on Saturdays. (We are not open on other days, and close at 1200 h on Saturdays.)

We open from 0900–1200 h only on Saturdays. (We are closed from 0900 to 1200 h on other days.)

When words are misplaced in conversation listeners take our intended meaning not only from what we say but also from the context, the intonation and the accompanying facial expressions, but we should still try to convey each message clearly in words that cannot be misunderstood. When using the word *only*, whether writing or speaking, it is worth taking the trouble to ensure that what you say does express precisely what you mean (see Table 5.1).

Other words that must be used with care, or ambiguity may result, include: *this*, *that* and *it*; *he*, *him*, *his*, *she* and *her*; *former* and *latter*; and *other* and *another*. For example, consider the use of the words *he*, *him* and *his* in the following sentence from a newspaper: 'A burglar who stabbed a man to

Table 5.1 Only: a word out of place

Cover this table with a sheet of paper, then uncover the first column and for the first five entries consider where the word *only* should be placed to convey the meaning you think the author probably intended.

What the authors wrote	Suggested improvement
The words 'no doubt' should only be used if the idea of certainty is to be conveyed.	The words 'no doubt' should be used only if the idea of certainty . . .
I can only write well when I know what I want to say.	I can write well only when . . .
She only made one journey which aroused the interest of detectives.	Only one of her journeys aroused the detectives' interest.
This bond is only available to members.	This bond is available only to members.
Cheques can only be accepted if . . .	Cheques can be accepted only if . . .
We should not be forced to spend time considering where precisely to place the word only . . . but to place it in a position that may spoil the meaning is bad.	Take care to place the word only where it will not spoil the meaning.

death when he found him breaking into his garden shed was jailed for life yesterday.'

The words *he* and *his* in this extract must refer to the man who died, and the word *him* to the burglar. To make the meaning clear at first reading, if necessary a noun should be repeated: 'A burglar who stabbed a man to death when found breaking into the man's garden shed was jailed for life yesterday.'

Repeat a word if it is the right word

The use of a word twice in a sentence, or several times in a paragraph, or many times on one page, may interrupt the smooth flow of language. This is why experienced writers try to avoid such undue repetition. But so-called elegant variation can be overdone.

For example, in a radio commentary on a game of baseball or football, a team may be described as the home side or as the visitors, and may also be referred to by its official name, by its nickname, by the colour of its shirts, and by the name of the ground on which it plays. As a result, to follow the commentary, before the game starts a listener has to know quite a lot about both teams.

To ensure that you are understood, it is best when referring to a spade to call it a spade. You may also repeat a word to emphasise a point. For example, in the last paragraph the word *by* is used four times in one sentence – to draw attention to each of the items in a list – although only the first *by* is actually needed to make sense.

In a talk you could place additional emphasis on the word repeated, by your intonation, by your facial expression, and, if you felt so inclined, by beating on the table with your fist!

Emphasise important points

Deliberate repetition can be especially effective in speech – when a word can be repeated to help you emphasise a succession of important points. The word repeated captures attention by the way you say it: first *by* a pause before the word and then *by* the intonation. For even greater effect, you could say: *by* (a) . . . , *by* (b) . . . , and *by* (c) . . .

Emphasis, which is achieved in many ways, is important in all communications and is present whether or not the speaker or writer is in control. But you can emphasise important points effectively only if you know how to make them stand out from the necessary supporting detail.

Beginnings and endings are important (in a talk, the introduction and conclusion). In a short contribution to a discussion, in making perhaps just one point, your first and last words capture most attention. In planning a longer contribution, a presentation or a talk, you have to decide on the number of main points you intend to make. Then you signal each main point first by a pause, which like a paragraph break in written composition helps to emphasise that one topic has been dealt with and it is time to start thinking about the next, and then by your first words after the pause which make clear your new topic.

So, in dealing with each topic, use your first and last words to convey information or to make connections – to help listeners understand your message and follow your train of thought.

An effective way to emphasise a difference between two sides of an argument or between two ways of considering an occurrence or event is to place two thoughts in opposition (in antithesis, see *Be persuasive*, page 40). The result may be apt, brief and memorable: for example, the six words 'To be, or not to be?' in Shakespeare's *Hamlet*; and Neil Armstrong's ten words as he stepped on to the moon in 1963, 'One small step for man, one giant leap for mankind.'

A listener's attention can also be captured and held by saying things in threes, as in each line of this anonymous nursery rhyme:

Baa, baa, black sheep,
Have you *any* wool?
Yes sir, yes sir, *three* bags full;
One for the master, and *one* for the dame, and *one* for the little boy
Who lives *down* the lane.

In the children's story 'The *Three* Little Pigs' the wolf *huffed* and *puffed* and *blew* the house down. The fairy godmother in a pantomime always grants three wishes; when appreciation is to be shown people are always asked to give three cheers; and there are many jokes about the three . . . , but did you ever hear one about the four . . . ?

Well-known advice on the development of interpersonal skills is: *see* no evil, *hear* no evil and *speak* no evil (or, in Yorkshire dialect in England, to see all, hear all and say nowt). It is no accident that in ancient times there were three Graces; that the Christian god is described as the Father, Son and Holy Ghost; that Shakespeare in *The Merchant of Venice* requires those seeking the hand of Portia to choose one from three caskets, and in *Henry V* causes the king to speak of 'This few, this happy few, this band of brothers' and to proclaim 'God for England, Harry and St George'.

Saying things in threes encourages people to anticipate what is to be said next (facilitates audience participation), gives them pleasure when they turn out to be right, and helps them to remember what has been said. Apt phrases may be remembered long after they were spoken, as are: the call in France in the 1760s for 'liberty, equality and . . . ', the promise in the United States of America in 1863 of 'government of the people, by the people, for . . . '; and the acknowledgement in Britain in 1940 of 'so much, owed by so many, to . . . '. These words are memorable not only because of the thoughts expressed and their presentation but also because they were appropriate: addressed to the right people, in the right place, at the right time.

Another way to emphasise your main points, fix them in people's minds, and add interest in a discussion, presentation or talk, is to include effective demonstrations or visual aids (see page 77). Indeed, many speakers rely too much on visual aids. They do not think enough about their choice and use of words.

Express your own thoughts

People who do not know what to say or have too few words at their command may use the wrong word (see chapter 4) or fall back on so-called hackneyed phrases (for example: *in pushing back the frontiers of knowledge,*

Table 5.2 Some idiomatic expressions

Instead of this	Say this
different kettle of fish	another matter
bury the hatchet	make peace
explore every avenue	consider all possibilities
lay one's cards on the table	make one's intentions clear
let the cat out of the bag	break a confidence
oil the wheels	facilitate
pull the other leg	Don't expect me to believe that.
play one's cards close to the chest	keep one's thoughts to oneself
spill the beans	fail to keep a secret
split hairs	quibble
work against time	try to finish on time

last but not least, at the end of the day, in the last analysis, and *all things being equal,* we hope to *see the light at the end of the tunnel.* George Orwell (1946), in his essay 'Politics and the English Language', complained that as soon as certain topics are raised people start to use such hackneyed phrases instead of taking the trouble to use words of their own choosing to convey their meaning precisely.

Idiomatic expressions (see Table 5.2) which have a special meaning that is not clear from the words used, are also best avoided: not only because, like hackneyed expressions, they make less impact than would a fresh turn of phrase, but also because they may be misunderstood by some people. It is best to choose words you expect your audience to understand and use them to express your own thoughts, in your own words, as clearly and simply as you can.

Use only necessary words

Unlike the novelist who is trying to paint pictures with words, leaving much to the reader's imagination, your intention when speaking in tutorials and seminars is to convey information without decoration: to express your thoughts as clearly and simply as you can.

Try not to use two words if only one is needed. In particular, never qualify words that have only one meaning (see Table 5.3). Facts, for example, are things known to be true (verified past events, things observed and recorded as data). So it is wrong to say that the evidence points to the fact, or that someone has got the facts wrong; and to speak of the actual facts is to say the same thing twice (see Table 5.4).

Table 5.3 Some words that should not be qualified

Don't say this	Say this
deliberately chosen	chosen
cylindrical in shape	cylindrical
a categorical denial	a denial
actual experience	experience
past experience	experience
an actual fact	a fact
hard facts	facts
completely full	full
green in colour	green
realistic justification	justification
absolutely perfect	perfect
almost perfect	slightly imperfect
quite possible	possible
very true	true
not actually true	untrue

Although a summarising or qualifying phrase may help to make things clear (see also *Use comment words and connecting words*, page 70), any unnecessary words are a smoke screen that can only obscure your meaning. A well-constructed sentence should have neither too many words nor too few; each word should be there for a purpose.

Fowler and Fowler (1906) and Quiller-Couch (1916) advised those who use language as an instrument for expressing and not concealing thought: (a) to prefer the short word to the long (see Table 4.2); (b) to prefer concrete nouns (names of things you can touch and see) to abstract nouns such as *aspect, condition, degree, experience* and *persuasion* (see also Table 5.5); (c) to prefer transitive verbs (that strike their object) and use them in the active voice (see Table 5.6); and (d) to prefer the direct word to the circumlocution (see Tables 5.7 and 5.8).

Orwell (1946), writing about public speaking, added: (e) be positive, especially avoid double negatives such as *not unlikely* for *possible*; (f) prefer your own well-chosen words to a hackneyed phrase or to any familiar (well-worn) metaphor, simile or other figure of speech; and (g) prefer everyday English words to foreign phrases and specialist terms.

Table 5.4 Tautology: saying the same thing twice using different words

Cover this table with a sheet of paper, then uncover column one and suggest which word or words should be deleted in each entry.

Don't say this	Say this
combined together	combined
congregated together	congregated
each individual person	each person
in actual fact	in fact
postponed to a later date	postponed
refer back	refer
still in use today	still in use
these ones	these
one after another in succession	in succession
an extra added bonus	a bonus
a complete monopoly	a monopoly
We are currently	We are
We are currently engaged in the process of	We are . . .
in my own personal opinion	in my opinion
advance planning	planning
different reasons	reasons
in equal halves	in halves
continue to remain	remain
linked together	linked
co-operate with each other	co-operate
ask the question whether	ask whether

Table 5.5 Some words to watch as indicators of jargon

Words to watch[a]	Instead of this	Say this
area	He worked in London as a physiotherapist after finishing a degree course in the same area.	He worked in London as a physiotherapist after graduating in this subject.
basis	on a regular basis on a part-time basis	regularly part-time
case	in the case of corporate presentations	for corporate presentations

Table 5.5 continued

Words to watch[a]	Instead of this	Say this
character	In establishments of a workshop rather than a factory character, . . .	In workshops, . . .
context	in a learning support context	to support learning
currently	We are currently making . . .	We are making . . .
environment	in a business environment	in business
experience	facilitate their learning experience	help them learn
fact	You are in fact quite correct. As a matter of fact, we are . . .	You are right. We are . . .
field	The police have entered the field of passive sniffing dogs. In the field of agriculture[b] . . .	The police are using dogs for passive drug-detection. In agriculture . . .
level	at the grass roots level at the management level policies at a national level and at a local level	basically in management national and local policies
nature	showers light in nature	light showers
	This problem of plagiarism is global in nature, causing problems for all universities.	Plagiarism is a problem in all universities.
process	throughout the writing process the process of consultation the peace process	while writing consultations negotiations
situation	in the job interview situation in a formal speaking situation working towards a unanimous situation	in a job interview in a talk trying to agree
spectrum	people from opposite ends of the age spectrum	both very old and very young people
time	at this precise moment in time	now

Notes
a   Many indicators of jargon are abstract nouns.
b   Latin, *agri cultura*, culture of a field (see also Table 5.7)

Table 5.6 Prefer the active voice to the passive voice*

Instead of this	Say this
These notes should be read before completing this form.	Read these notes before you complete this form.
Your driving licence must be enclosed with this form.	Enclose your driving licence with this form.
The following results were obtained.	We obtained the following results.
A mass of papers has to be read.	We all have to read a mass of papers.
My colleagues are asked to . . .	I ask my colleagues to . . .
Hopefully . . .	I hope . . . (*or* We hope . . .)
Smoking is not permitted.	No smoking.

Note
* Active voice: where the subject of the sentence is the agent of the action.
Passive voice: where the subject is the recipient of the action.

Reasons for verbosity

Circumlocution, verbosity – gobbledegook – surplusage – this habit of excess in the use of words, which makes communication more difficult than it should be, is well established in the speech of many educated people. As long ago as 1667, in his *History of the Royal Society*, Thomas Sprat wrote that

> of all the Studies of men, nothing may be sooner obtain'd than this vicious abundance of *Phrase*, this trick of *Metaphors*, this volubility of *Tongue*, which makes so great a noise in the World. But I spend words in vain; for the evil is now so inveterate, that it is hard to know whom to *blame*, or where to begin to *reform*. We all value one another so much, upon this beautiful deceit; and labour for so long after it, in the years of our education: that we cannot but ever after think kinder of it, than it deserves.

Tautology, circumlocution, ambiguity and verbosity arise from ignorance of the exact meaning of words, and from lack of care in the use of words. Also, people may use too few words when they speak, or too many words when they write, if they have not considered the difference between speech and writing.

In a conversation or discussion we may use more or fewer words than we would in writing. On the one hand, we use words to separate important ideas, we repeat things for emphasis, and we correct ourselves – because we are thinking as we talk – in an attempt to achieve greater precision. The extra words give listeners time to think. On the other hand, in conversation we take short cuts – leaving out words – and so use fewer words than would be needed in writing. This is possible because as we talk we also communicate without words: (a) by meaningful silences; and (b) by body language (see page 10) in which, in the words of Marie Lloyd's music hall song of 1912, 'Every little movement has a meaning of its own'. We see when we have said enough. Thomas Hardy, in *Far From the Madding Crowd* (1874), emphasised the power of thoughts communicated without words:

> 'Good morning.' His tone was so utterly removed from all she had expected as a beginning. It was lowness and quiet accentuated: an emphasis of deep meanings, their form at the same time being scarcely expressed. Silence has sometimes a remarkable power of showing itself as the disembodied soul of feeling wandering without its carcass, and it is then more impressive than speech . . .
>
> So the chatter was all on her side. There is a loquacity that tells nothing, which was Bathsheba's; and there is a silence which says much: that was Gabriel's . . .
>
> Those who have the power of reproaching in silence may find it a means more effective than words. There are accents in the eye which are not on the tongue, and more tales come from pale lips than enter the ear. It is both the grandeur and the pain of the remoter moods that they avoid the pathway of sound. Boldwood's look was unanswerable.

In writing, to allow for the lack of direct contact with the reader, enough words must be used to convey the intended meaning. Emphasis can usually be made without repetition, and necessary pauses come from punctuation marks and paragraph breaks. In speaking, as in writing, use words with which you are familiar and try to match your style to the occasion and to the needs of those present; but recognise that good spoken English is not the same as good written English (see page 74): a good talk that is recorded and then typed verbatim is unlikely to make good prose.

Similarly, a document that is dictated is unlikely to make a good impression unless it is revised in typescript. Few people are able to dictate anything other than a short routine communication so that it reads well and conveys the intended meaning unless they are prepared to spend time converting the typescript into good prose. But most people, if they take the trouble, can: (a) write better than they normally talk – because in writing they have more time for thought and the opportunity to revise their work;

and (b) deliver a better talk if they write exactly what they intend to say (see pages 83–5) and then speak from concise notes (see pages 100–2).

Apart from lack of care, there are other reasons why many people are grandiloquent and verbose. Some seem to think that restatement in longer words is explanation. Some are trying to make a little knowledge go a long way. And some may even be trying to obscure meaning because they have nothing to say, or do not wish to commit themselves.

Wordiness may also result from affectation: from the studied avoidance of simplicity. Some people seem to think, when they have to make a speech or dictate an official letter, that they must use a more pompous language than they would in everyday conversation or in a letter to a friend (for example, see Tables 5.7 and 5.8). Too often, as Orwell (1946) complained, short words are replaced by phrases (for example, *about* by *with respect to or having regard to*) and the ends of sentences are saved from anticlimax by resounding commonplaces (for example, *greatly to be desired, cannot be left out of account, a development to be expected in the near future, deserving of serious consideration*, and *brought to a satisfactory conclusion*). The words *categorical* (see Table 5.3), *individual* (see Table 5.4), *currently, process, situation*

Table 5.7 The use of a phrase when one word would serve the purpose better

Instead of this	Say this
in connection with	about
with reference to	about
with regard to	about
all of	all
in spite of the fact that	although
on account of the fact that	because
in view of the fact that	because
take into consideration	consider
during the course of	during
utilise for sustenance	eat
few in number	few
for the purpose of	for
a large proportion of	many
in the vicinity of	near
in attendance	present
a percentage of	some
at an early date	soon
of the opinion that	thinks

Table 5.8 Circumlocution: the use of many words where fewer would be better

Cover this table with a sheet of paper, then uncover column one and for each entry suggest how the meaning could be better expressed in fewer words.

Instead of this	Say this
How we speak depends upon the speech communities we are actually operating in at the time. (16 words)	How we speak depends on whom we are with. (9 words)
This is the first time we have stepped into the field of passive indicating dogs and it is a new tool we can use to address the problem of drugs. (30 words)	This is the first time we have used passive indicating dogs for drug detection. (14 words)
They are without any sanitary arrangements whatsoever.	They are without sanitation.
The committee was obviously cognisant of the problem.	The committee was aware of the problem.
by any actual person in particular	by anyone in particular
delegated downwards to	delegated to
at local neighbourhood level	in neighbourhoods
for more than seven decades	for over seventy years*
for a further period of ten years	for another ten years
The roads were limited in mileage.	There were few roads.
He was of the opinion that . . .	He thought that . . .
I would have said	I think
Have a listen.	Listen.
More importantly	More important
Up until now	Until now
located in the town centre	in the town centre
housed in a new building	in a new building
situated in parkland	in parkland

Note
* If possible, be precise: say how long.

(see Table 5.5) and *utilise* (see Table 5.7), for example, are used to dress up simple statements and give an air of scientific impartiality to biased judgements . . . Foreign words and expressions are used to give an air of culture and elegance.

Use comment words and connecting words

In practising an economy of words, do not make the mistake of using too few words. As well as the words needed to convey meaning, help listeners to follow your train of thought by including comment words (for example, *clearly*, *even*, *as expected* and *unexpected*) and connecting words (for example, *first*, *second*, *then*, *therefore*, *hence*, *however*, *on the contrary*, *moreover*, *as a result*, *nevertheless*, *similarly*, *so*, *thus*, *but*, *on the one hand* and *on the other hand*).

Some introductory and connecting phrases (for example, 'As mentioned earlier . . . ' and 'From this you will see that . . . '), which would usually be superfluous in writing, may be needed when speaking – to provide reminders and to ensure that all present appreciate why what you are saying is relevant. Your message should be neither obscured by a haze of superfluous words nor deprived of words needed to give it strength. The rule must be to use the number of words needed to convey each thought precisely (without ambiguity), and to ensure that brevity is not achieved at the expense of accuracy, clarity, interest and coherence.

With reference to value for money, and to an economy of words, when University of Cambridge undergraduates heard that Rudyard Kipling was to be paid £1 per word for an article in *The Times* and wrote asking him to send one of his best words, he replied 'Thanks', and when the opera singer Adelena Patti was asked if she thought it right that she should be paid more for one performance than the president of the United States earned in a whole year, she replied: 'Does he sing?' Whatever your purpose, when speaking, if you intend to be widely understood you too will usually want to convey your message as clearly and simply as you can.

Improve your performance

Editing the work of others

It is easier to check and reflect on your use of words when writing than when speaking, because a document can be checked and if necessary can be revised. So the best way to learn to express your thoughts more effectively is to try to improve your writing. As a student you should also be developing your ability to read critically.

Look critically at letters and memoranda you receive from business people. You will probably find it easier to recognise long words that could be replaced by shorter words, phrases that should be deleted, and sentences that are verbose, when you read other people's writing than when you try to revise your own. However, after editing the writing of others (as suggested in Tables 5.7 and 5.8) you will start to take more care with your own choice and use of words both when writing and when speaking.

Writing précis and summaries

Because it is easier to condense other people's writing than your own, practice in preparing and revising précis and summaries will help you to develop a concise and direct style that is appropriate for most of the communications, spoken or written, that you prepare as a student or in other employment.

Writing a précis is a test of comprehension and an exercise in reduction, in which the essential meaning of a composition is retained – but without ornament and without the details. The author's meaning should therefore be conveyed in your own words – and in fewer words. As part of a course in Communication Skills, a class of students could be asked (a) to prepare a précis of an article from a journal, working alone; and then (b) to try to agree as to which of the author's words could be omitted in the précis.

For practice in writing a summary, select an article relevant to your own work from a recent issue of a magazine or journal in which authors' summaries are published. Before looking at the author's summary, read the article carefully, listing the main points, and then prepare your own summary. Note that a summary should be much shorter than a précis. It should include only the author's main points; so preparing a summary is a good test of your ability to recognise these main points, and to report them in a few well-chosen words.

When you are satisfied with your summary, look at the author's own summary. Do you agree with the author's choice of the most important points? Has the author used more words than are needed? Have you?

Listening to yourself

Most people find hearing themselves speak an interesting and salutary experience. If you record a conversation (for example, a phone call) or the whole of a self-help group discussion, you will be able not only to hear the sound of your own voice as others hear it, but also to consider your choice and use of words. You may also realise that you use some words and phrases out of habit rather than to convey meaning (for example, ending sentences with 'right', 'like', 'sort of', 'you know'). Good listening!

6 Preparing a talk or presentation

Most students are expected to give short talks or presentations as part of their coursework; and applicants for employment may be expected to give a short presentation as part of an employer's selection procedures. Then, in any profession, people in responsible positions may be asked, for example, to give instruction in a training course, to organise a presentation relating to new developments or new requirements, or to address a larger audience. Even in such different situations, the qualities required of a speaker are the same: knowledge of the subject, enthusiasm, simplicity in the use of language, and sincerity.

A *presentation* is a special kind of talk: an exercise in persuasion involving one or more presenters, in which something new is presented to an invited audience for consideration. For a student this is likely to be a new topic, not previously considered on the course, in relation to which it would be necessary to introduce the subject, define essential terms, persuade those present of its relevance and importance as part of the course, and provide a basis for discussion. Each presentation, having a limited objective, should be complete in itself – but should leave the audience interested, impressed, ready to discuss, and wanting to know more.

In a *talk* or *lecture* delivered to an audience, on a subject of common interest, the speaker is the composer and conductor as well as the performer. The talk may be an opportunity, for example: to provide a foundation for independent study or research (to introduce); to present a subject and view it as a whole (to further stimulate interest); to present facts and opinions not readily available elsewhere (to inform); to develop an argument (to persuade); or, as in many lectures, to draw attention to important points, contradictions and uncertainties (to stimulate discussion and further thought). A talk or lecture is less formal than a speech, and it is not usually the speaker's intention to stir the listeners' emotions.

Whether it is called a presentation or a talk, you are advised to prepare to address an audience, as you would prepare to write an essay or any other written composition, in four stages. Always: (a) *think* about what listeners need to know; (b) *plan* how best to tell them; (c) *write* a draft of your talk; and (d) *check* that, preferably speaking from notes, you can deliver your talk at the right pace and with appropriate emphasis in the time available. Then, if necessary, revise your notes.

Think

Before any talk or presentation, whether speaking alone or as part of a team, there are six things you must know.

1   *What* exactly are you to speak about (a title or precise terms of reference)?
2   *Who* will be your audience (their age, background, expectations and interests)?
3   *Why* (for a lecture) have you been invited to speak to this audience, or *why* (for a presentation) have these people been invited to listen to you?
4   *When* are you to speak (date and time)?
5   *How* much time is available (how many minutes for your talk, and how many for questions)?
6   *Where* are you to speak? You need to know the place, *how* large an audience is expected, the size of the room, and the facilities available.

If you are one of a team making a presentation, *you must* discuss and agree what exactly each member of the team is to contribute, and *you must* have at least one rehearsal to ensure: (a) that each contribution can be completed in an agreed time; (b) that the different contributions are in an effective order and are well co-ordinated; and (c) that the whole presentation runs smoothly and ends on time.

People can proceed at their own pace when reading. If something is not clear immediately they can stop and try to work things out. But if listeners are trying to understand what has just been said, they will not be concentrating on what is being said next. That is to say, in a talk everyone must understand all that is said – at first hearing. The speaker must ensure, by adequate preparation, that all is right from the start.

Decide what your audience needs to know

To whom will you be speaking? What are their interests? What prior knowledge, if any, can you assume to be shared by everyone likely to be present? What do they need to know? What are their likely feelings about the subject of your talk? Can you anticipate any opposition to your views? How well do they know you? What do they expect of you? How do you expect them to benefit from your talk? Can you anticipate questions that they may ask?

Ask yourself such questions, about your audience and about the subject of your talk, to stimulate your thoughts. As you think, make notes, spreading key words, phrases and whole sentences over a sheet of paper or over your computer screen; or write each note on a separate index card).

Consider your purpose

Why are you giving this talk? Do you intend, for example, to encourage, to entertain, to explain, to inform, to inspire, to instruct, to persuade? What can you achieve in the time available? In one sentence, what will be your message?

Plan

Design your message to suit your purpose

1   If you have agreed to talk on a particular subject, keep to your terms of reference.
2   Decide on a limited number of main points that you must make in the limited time available. Do not attempt too much. Your purpose should not be to impress your audience with how much you know about the subject but to tell them just what they need to know so that they can understand and will remember your message.
3   Number these points or re-arrange them in an appropriate order (as you would before an important telephone call or when preparing a topic outline for any important written communication).
4   If possible, put your plan on one side overnight, or for a few days, to give yourself time for reflection and second thoughts. Then check that each point is essential in relation to your purpose.

Consider the differences between speaking and writing

You are advised to write out any talk to be delivered to an audience in full, to ensure you can say all that should be included, in an appropriate order and with any necessary aids, in the time available. However, be aware of the differences between spoken and written language.

If you have written an essay or report on the subject of your talk, remember that speaking is not the same as writing. A good composition, prepared for silent reading, will not make a good talk if it is simply read aloud. Therefore: (a) if you must read your talk, write so that it will sound well when read aloud; but (b) if you can, having written your talk, it is best to speak from notes.

It is said that the British actor Alec Guinness deleted many words from a film script, saying that he could convey the message by facial expressions alone. 'He could steal a scene with his back', said John Le Carré, author of *Tinker, Tailor, Soldier, Spy*. On the same subject, the American actor Clint Eastwood, a man of few words in the film *For a Few Dollars More*, said: 'You can do a lot without doing a lot, if you see what I mean'.

In giving a talk it is important to remember that you are communicating with your audience even when you are not speaking. Reading a talk reduces this non-verbal communication because every time you look down at a prepared script, you lose eye contact with your audience and they cannot see your facial expressions.

In conversation, when responding to others you compose your thoughts as you speak and may need, for example, to rephrase what you have just said to clarify important points when you see that someone looks puzzled or obviously does not follow your argument. Because you are thinking and responding to the reactions of others, you are unlikely to speak as fast as you could if reading a prepared speech. This is another reason why simply reading a prepared text, without the pauses and changes of emphasis that are part of normal conversation, does not result in a good talk.

Even if something is very well written, for example a play by Shakespeare, the beauty of the language and the dramatic effect of a speech is lost in a too rapid delivery or if necessary meaningful pauses are omitted. Charles Macklin (McLoughlin), a leading eighteenth-century Irish actor, said, regarding the use of silence for effect, that he had three kinds of pause: his first a short and light affair, like a comma; his second longer and more important, like a semicolon; and his grand pause even longer and more forceful, almost a full stop, as he kept his audience waiting for the punch line.

In preparing a talk, consider when periods of silence are needed by your audience. For example, you will need to allow time for people to look at any handout or visual aid without the distracting effect of your voice – after or before you explain what especially you would like them to note. You will need to pause after making each of your main points to allow people time for reflection, and you will need short pauses for emphasis after some important sentences (which you may underline in your notes).

Whereas most scholarly writing is in standard English (using complete words – as in a dictionary), in a talk you would probably use the contractions that come naturally in conversation and when writing to close friends: for example, *don't* (for *do not*), *it's* (for *it is* or *it has*), *won't* (for *will not*), and *who's* (for *who is* or *who has*). However, for most purposes, and for most audiences, it is best to avoid slang (see page 5).

In writing you might explain: 'This is what was done . . . ' (in the passive voice, see Table 5.6), but in a talk you would use the first or second person: 'I did this . . . ', 'We did this . . . ' or 'As you know . . . '.

In scholarly writing rhetorical questions are usually inappropriate, but they may be useful in a talk to make listeners think about what you have just said ('What can we conclude?'), or start thinking about what you plan to say next ('What could we do about that?').

Communicate your purpose

Whereas the reader does not require your plan (see page 74), listeners do need a map or guide to help them find the way. Some introductory phrases that would be superfluous in writing may help listeners to understand how your talk is organised, and how it is progressing. They serve the same purpose as the headings and sub-headings in a written communication, telling listeners what comes next or reminding them of important points already made. For example: 'As the title of my talk indicates, . . . ', 'So far we have seen that . . . ', 'The next thing I want you to consider is . . . ', 'As I have already emphasised . . . '. And, when you are sure you are just about to end, you could say: 'To summarise, . . . ' or 'In conclusion, . . . ' or 'I leave you with this message . . . '.

Also, apart from the way you choose to express your thoughts, remember that listeners cannot assimilate all the detail that is needed in some written reports but has no place in a talk. Most inexperienced speakers, and many experienced speakers who have not taken enough trouble in planning their talks, attempt to cover too many main points, use too many visual aids, and include too much supporting detail. That is to say, they attempt to do more than can be done well in the time available. As a result, some things are insufficiently explained, little is likely to be remembered, and few will be able to recall the main points accurately – even if they tried to make notes.

Repetition is usually undesirable in a written communication, because readers can move forward at their own pace and if necessary can read the words more than once; but listeners, without repetition, do not have a second chance. In a talk repetition also helps listeners to recognise and remember the most important points.

So in a talk you may, for example, (a) state the title; (b) say briefly what aspect of the subject you will consider and what each part of your talk will be about; (c) state the main point you want to make at the start of each part of your talk; (d) explain each main point with some supporting evidence, and give an example; (e) briefly rephrase what you have said, to ensure everyone understands each stage in your talk; (f) restate your main points towards the end of your talk so that they lead directly to your conclusions; and (g) provide a handout at the end of your talk. If your message is clearly stated in your introduction, and everything you say reinforces this message, a short final sentence may fix this message in your listeners' minds.

Do you need any audio-visual aids?

In a talk or presentation, well-chosen audio-visual aids: (a) add interest; and (b) provide variety – a change for your audience from just looking at you and listening to your voice. They (c) capture attention and may be remembered when much of what you say has been forgotten, and so *should be used only for your most important points*. They (d) help to hold attention if, for example, they are used in sequence as you develop an argument. They should complement your words, enabling you (e) to provide essential evidence (for example, in a table or graph) that could not be conveyed adequately with words alone.

Effective audio-visual aids may enable you to convey more information than would otherwise be possible, but because you must allow people to pay attention to them without the distracting sound of your voice *you must plan to say less*.

Prepare any necessary stores or equipment you will need during your talk. Plan any demonstration that will reinforce your words and add interest (for example, the use of a specimen or model).

If you plan to include an *audio aid*, record just the extract you require, so that when you are ready to use it you only have to switch on. But check the recording in the room you will be using for the talk, to make sure the sound is good. Then remember to wind the extract back to the start. Appropriate sounds can add interest to a talk, but there is much more that can go wrong with audio aids than with visual aids (as a result, for example, of badly placed loud speakers), and you might prefer not to use them unless you have expert help.

Decide exactly when you will use any demonstrations, handouts or audio-visual aids needed to support your words – so that they do support your spoken words and are not visible as a distraction when you are trying to interest your audience in something else. And if you need to use more than one kind of visual aid (for example, a model and slides, or slides and overhead projector transparencies) try to finish with one before you start using the other – so that you do not have to move back and forth between the two.

Decide which words are most important (these may be main headings or key words underlined in your notes). Write any words that may be new to some members of your audience in capital letters in your notes so that you will remember to write them in large, clear, capital letters on a chalkboard, marker-board or flip chart when you first use them in your talk. Otherwise, a *visual aid* should not be just words, which would help only those who could not hear you speak, unless, for example, you need to provide concise instructions (see Figure 6.1) or an important definition – and then allow time for note-taking without the sound of your voice.

Remember (a) that people have come to your talk to hear you speak, not to watch you read aloud words displayed on a screen; and (b) that you cannot look at anyone if you are looking at the screen. Also, whereas people can listen together, with the speaker in control, they read at different speeds – and the speaker loses control of the pace of delivery. So speak your words. Use pictures for just the things that you want people to see – and to reduce the number of words needed to convey your message.

Arrange your visual aids for a talk in order and check them, if possible by sitting in the back row of the room to be used for the talk, to ensure that everyone will be able to see them clearly and read any numbers or words.

TO HARD-BOIL AN EGG

(1) Cover the egg with cold water

(2) Bring to the boil

(3) Simmer for 5 minutes

(4) Cool in cold water

The white will be white and the yolk golden

Perfect!

Figure 6.1 A guide to the arrangement of words on a visual aid. When words are most appropriate, include a title, and up to 32 words of text – but no more than 8 lines of text (in a 4 × 3 slide) and no more than 8 words per line. Note that a full stop should not be used after the title, and it is not usually necessary to use other punctuation marks. However, remember that people have come to listen to you speak, not to read your words on visual aids! So when choosing visual aids always prefer pictures to words.

If you decide to use slides, consider when best to use them. If you are using a slide projector it will be necessary to switch off the room lights. Then it would be disturbing to everyone if you switched them on and off repeatedly; but if the lights are off all the time you cannot maintain eye contact with your audience and they cannot make notes. So, try to show the slides in one batch. Talk first and then show your slides; or use the slides to provide a break in a long talk or to separate the body of your talk from the summary and conclusions. Consider these possibilities even if you are using a liquid crystal display (LCD) projector with your visual aids on a disk. What is best on one occasion may be inappropriate on another.

If using a slide projector, include a duplicate of any slide you intend to refer to twice, so that you do not have to display other slides a second time – in reverse order – as you try to find the one you need, and then a third time in correct order, as you go forward to find your next slide. It is also best to include blank slides wherever necessary, so that you needn't continue to display, until you are ready for the next slide, a visual aid that you no longer want people see.

If you use any aid that is to occupy a few minutes (for example, a specimen, a model or a film) consider using it about half way through your talk, perhaps before or after a short break. Your first words will then provide an introduction, the visual aid will support what you have said in the body of your talk, and it could be followed by any comments you need to make, by your conclusions, and by questions and discussion. For further advice on preparing visual aids, see Chapter 7, *Preparing visual aids*.

Do you need any handouts?

When preparing a talk or presentation, decide whether or not you should provide any handouts. Most people are pleased to accept handouts and may file them, but they may not read them.

To increase the chances of your handouts being read, (a) try to fit the material for each handout on one side of an A4 page, so that nobody will be put off by its length – and it can be inserted in a file in the most appropriate place; and (b) try to summarise the main point of your talk (your message), or the points you particularly want people to remember, in a few words as part of an eye-catching illustration (as in many advertisements and cartoons).

Like any other communication, each handout should be dated and should include your name (or initials if more appropriate) and your address, so that you can be contacted by anyone who requires further information or would like to provide feedback.

For a series of talks it is helpful to distribute a list of titles in advance to all those expected to attend, or to provide a list as a handout at the start of the first talk. Otherwise, do not provide handouts before a talk unless they are needed at the beginning. If you do, some people may be looking at the handout when you are trying to interest them in something else.

You must have more than enough copies of any handout you intend to distribute during your talk (for example, a table of essential data including more words or numbers than would be acceptable in a visual aid). This is one reason why, well in advance, you need to know how many people are likely to attend. Include one copy of the handout in your notes, at the point where you will want people to refer to it, to remind you when to distribute copies to your audience. Similarly, if you prepare a handout for distribution after your talk (to provide any necessary detail that would have been inappropriate in the talk, such as a list of sources of further information), include a copy at the end of your notes to remind you to say that this handout is available.

Some speakers prepare handouts that are just notes on their talks. If they are giving a series of talks, especially, this discourages some people from making concise notes related to their own needs (which is, in itself, a rewarding activity, see page 24). If notes are provided as a matter of routine, some people will soon decide that they needn't listen and some that they needn't attend. For further advice on using handouts and visual aids, see pages 103–4.

Interest your audience

Instead of telling your audience that something you are about to say is interesting, try to make it interesting. This will depend on your own interest in the subject, and on: (a) your knowledge of the subject and your ability to select just what is relevant to this talk; (b) showing *this audience*, in your short introduction, that what you have to say is *relevant to their needs* – that it follows on from their existing interests or that it will help them in some other way; (c) meeting the audience's expectations in relation to the arrangement of your material by, for example, following the word *both* by *and*, not only by *but also*, either by *or*, and *first* by *second*, etc.; (d) using similar forms of expression to draw attention to similarities or to differences in content, as in 'At first we used . . . but now we use . . . '; (e) ensuring variety and simplicity in your delivery; (f) summarising, when necessary, to give people a second chance to grasp important points; (g) using appropriate audio-visual aids, so that people are not just sitting looking at you and listening to your voice; and (e) avoiding distractions.

People will listen most carefully, and will remember best, what you say in the first fifteen minutes of a talk; and thirty minutes with one person talking is enough for any listener.

You may begin by saying how you became interested in the subject (with appropriate acknowledgements) or by explaining the nature of your interest (the aspect you are to consider in this talk – which should also be clear from the title), so that no one expects more of you than you plan to deliver. But never begin with an apology. For example, never say that you are not really qualified to speak on this subject. Do any necessary background reading or research to make sure that you do know enough about the subject.

Some speakers like to begin with a joke, to put people at ease, but this is not usually appropriate in a presentation given as part of a college or university course. Even in situations when a joke might be appropriate, in a short talk telling the joke would occupy time that you might not be able to spare; and it may be difficult to find a new joke that matches both the occasion and the interests of your audience. A speaker does not get off to a good start if people feel obliged to laugh.

In a talk you may say, for example, what you observed, what you thought, how you investigated, what you discovered or concluded, what you plan to do or what you think should be done next. To retain the confidence of your audience, you must be positive and self-confident.

A well-planned thirty-minute talk, in *three parts* (see Table 6.1), may comprise the *beginning* – your introduction including a reference to your interests and to things familiar to your audience (5 minutes) – the *middle* – your main points (10 minutes), elaboration and visual aids (8 minutes) – and the *end* – your conclusions (2 minutes), and questions (5 minutes). Or it may comprise your message (3 minutes), the problem, evidence and your conclusions (16 minutes), repetition of your message (1 minute) and questions (5 minutes).

In a fifty-minute talk you should be able to say more, but not much more. There is a certain magic in the number seven (7 colours in a rainbow, 7 days in a week, 7 deadly sins, 7 wonders of the world), but five main points is perhaps as many as you would want the people in your audience to remember. So your talk could be in seven parts: your *introduction* (less than 10 minutes), *five topics*, each comprising a statement, an explanation and an analogy or example (7 minutes each), and your *conclusion* (less than 5 minutes).

Table 6.1 The three parts of a talk or presentation – related to its purpose

Beginning	Middle	End
To argue		
An observation	Further observations	Generalisation[a]
Generalisation	Examples	Expectation[b]
To inform		
Background	Present position	Prospects
History	Anything new	Consequences
Information	Explanation – examples	Conclusion
To instruct		
Say what to do	Explain – demonstrate	Watch them do it
To persuade		
Problem	Solution proposed	Its advantages
Difficulties	Need for change – possibilities	Recommendation
Change proposed	Reasons or need for change	Consequences
To report		
What went wrong	Why – lessons learned	Action taken

Notes
a   Inductive reasoning (arguing from particular instances or observations to generalisations).
b   Deductive reasoning which, if based on a true premise, should lead to a logical
    conclusion (applying a generalisation to a particular case).

Any questions?

Should you ask your audience any questions? If so, write them at appropriate points in your notes. Such questions are most likely to be needed in
a short presentation or in a training session, but rhetorical questions can be
useful in a longer talk – to keep everyone's attention.

For a longer talk, consider whether or not you would like to invite
questions from the audience (usually at the end of a talk). If you would, try
to anticipate questions that you are likely to be asked, especially about
anything you intend to say that is controversial, and make notes so that you
are prepared to give concise answers or can say where further information
is to be found. If you are not going to invite questions, try to ensure that in
your talk you do answer the questions you might have expected members of
this audience to ask (see page 74).

Write

Ronald Reagan (1990) in *An American Life* gave his five rules for public
speaking.

1   Use simple language.
2   Do not use a word with two syllables if a one-syllable word will do.
3   Prefer short sentences.
4   If you can, use an example: an example (or an analogy) is better than a sermon.
5   Audiences are made up of individuals, so speak as if you were talking to a few friends.

Write all you plan to say in full

Write what you intend to say, with appropriate headings for each main point and marginal notes to remind you when to use your visual aids. If you plan to talk for twenty-five minutes, you should write about 2,500 words (about ten sheets of A4 paper typed double spaced using one side only).

Read your script aloud to yourself, pausing where necessary (for example, where you plan to use a visual aid) to check: (a) that you have not written anything you would not say; (b) how much time you need to make each point, and (c) that you can complete the talk in the time allowed.

Whatever you have to say, it is important to recognise that any subject can be presented in whatever time is available. For example, you could describe a cucumber in one sentence, or give a more complete description in one short paragraph, but more than 750 words are used in the European Economic Community Regulation relating to the look of cucumbers supplied fresh to the consumer, at all market stages, including their curvature, colour and surface features; and a further thirty-four words to explain that, in addition: 'at stages following dispatch the products may show, in relation to the standards prescribed, a slight lack of freshness and turgescence and slight alteration due to their biological development and their tendency to perish' (EEC, 1988).

Similarly, the plot of a novel could be summarised on a postcard, condensed in a longer précis, abridged if considered too long for the intended audience, or printed complete as the author intended.

Prepare to speak from notes

Have the manuscript for your talk readily available, in case you need to refer to it, but unless you have to read it word for word it is best to speak from notes.

Make a note of each main point (topic) as a heading on a separate index card (to be used as a cue card) or at the top of a blank sheet of paper – with a few key words (as prompts to remind you of evidence, or of an example, or of a visual aid to be used at this stage in your talk), and a note of what the time should then be (in minutes from the start of your talk). The number of points you can make in the time available, and the amount of supporting detail required, will depend upon your audience.

Arrange your cards (or sheets of paper) in order. Then number them so that you start with any information that provides essential background, speak briefly and to the point about each topic, and arrive at your conclusion on time.

Check

Rehearse your talk

Rehearse your talk, speaking aloud to your image in a mirror or to a few friends, and referring only to your brief notes (one cue card or one sheet of paper for each topic).

1　Place your cue cards or your A4 sheets of notes next to your stop watch.
2　Start the stop watch as you pick up the first cue card or sheet of notes.
3　When you have finished with each cue card or sheet of notes put it well out of your way.
4　Check the time as you pause at the end of each topic, and pick up the next cue card or the next sheet of your notes.

Some speakers use an appropriate sequence of visual aids, instead of cue cards or other notes, with the result that: (a) they are reading words they intended their audience to read for themselves; (b) they are looking at the screen when they should be looking at their audience; (c) they may not remember to mention everything they intended to say; and (d) they do not find it easy to keep to time.

If friends help with your rehearsal, encourage them to ask questions, and to let you have any comments or suggestions. As when reviewing the draft of a written composition, it is helpful if a discerning and sympathetic critic, whose judgement you trust, says what went well (for example, communicating your main points with effective connections) and where there is room for improvement (for example, in making good important omissions, in correcting other mistakes or ambiguities, in cutting out unnecessary detail, in pointing out distracting mannerisms).

You would probably also find it a salutary experience to video-record your talk so that you can see and hear yourself speak. The first time you do this it may be discomforting as well as being instructive, but recognising the possibility of improvement is the first step towards improving your performance and mastering the techniques of public speaking.

Do you appear interested and enthusiastic? Is every word pronounced clearly? Is each of your main points made effectively? Do you make proper connections? Are you maintaining sufficient eye contact with your audience? Are you looking at your audience when they are looking at your visual aids? Are you pausing long enough after each of your main points?

Have you any gestures or expressions that you over-use (mannerisms) and were unaware of, which your audience will find distracting? For example, some speakers repeat the words *sort of*, *like* and *I mean*, and hesitate . . . *er* . . . so often as to distract attention from their message. Unwanted gestures, words and phrases may be a sign of inadequate preparation or nervousness. Some hesitations give a speaker time for thought. Some expressions – *you see*, *you know*, *all right* and *if you follow me* – may be attempts at confirmation.

Revise your notes for your talk

In the light of this trial make any changes that are needed to ensure that after a short introduction you will be able to make each of your main points forcefully, arrive at an effective conclusion, and answer a few questions, in the time available.

Then, during your talk, if you can, refer only to your brief notes – as reminders. If you can, *avoid reading a typescript or words displayed on your visual aids* (which people can read for themselves: see Figure 6.1). For most of the time, maintain the eye contact with your audience that is essential for an effective presentation.

Find out the size of the room to be used for your talk, so that you can ensure that everyone present will be able to see any demonstration and read the words on your visual aids.

The advice given in this chapter on how to prepare a talk or presentation is summarised in Table 6.2. For advice on preparing visual aids see chapter 7, and for advice on delivering a talk or presentation see chapter 8. If you follow this advice you will be well prepared.

Improve your performance

Using a computer when preparing a talk or presentation

Many who use a computer for word processing, for sending and receiving e-mail, and for obtaining information via the Internet, do not appreciate how they can use it in other ways to help them with their work – with software programs that may already be installed in their computers. Although a program was developed to help users perform a particular

Table 6.2 How to prepare a talk or presentation

THINK	1	Consider your title or terms of reference.
	2	Define the purpose and scope of your talk, if these are not clearly stated in the title.
	3	Decide what everyone in your audience needs to know.
	4	Allocate the time available for your preparations to thinking, planning, writing and revising.
	5	Make notes of relevant information and ideas.
PLAN	6	Prepare a topic outline.
	7	Underline the points you will emphasise.
	8	Decide on an effective beginning.
	9	Number the topics, arranging them in an appropriate order.
	10	Decide how to end.
	11	Decide what help you will need with the preparation of visual aids and liaise with the people concerned.
WRITE	13	If your first draft is hand-written, use wide-lined A4 paper with a 25 mm margin. Write one paragraph on each sheet, and write on one side only, so that – as with a word processor – you can revise your paragraphs or change their order easily.
	14	If possible, put other tasks on one side and work where you will be free from interruption.
	15	Use your topic outline as a guide.
	16	Use effective headings and keep to the point.
	17	Try to complete your draft at one sitting, using the first words that come to mind.
CHECK	18	Does your draft read well? Is it well balanced?
	19	Are the main points sufficiently emphasised?
	20	Is anything essential missing?
	21	Is the meaning of each sentence clear and correct?
	22	Does your use of words match the needs of your audience?
	23	If you can, after revising your draft put it on one side for a while to give yourself time for reflection.
	24	Read it again to see if you are still satisfied that it is the best you can do in the time available.
PRACTISE	25	Read your talk aloud, pausing where necessary for effect and where you will need time to display your visual aids, to check that you can complete it and answer a few questions in the time available.
	26	Try to summarise your talk by writing key words, phrases and important sentences on separate index cards, so that you can use these notes as reminders instead of reading your talk.
	27	Practise your talk, with a few friends as your audience, speaking from your notes and supported by your visual aids.
	28	Revise your talk, if necessary, in the light of this trial.

task (for example, word processing) it may be installed as part of a suite containing other programs developed to help users with other tasks (for example, with preparing and delivering presentations, with preparing and using spreadsheets and with drawing diagrams and charts); and each of these programs may have capabilities that overlap with those of the others.

With appropriate software it is easy to prepare: (a) a topic outline for a talk; (b) speaker's notes; (c) visual aids for use during a talk as over-head projector transparencies or as slides; and (d) handouts providing further details – for distribution after a talk. Slides (actually images stored electronically on a disk) can be prepared with or without a background colour and design; and both visual aids and handouts can include words alone, tables, charts or other artwork – including photographs. However, care should be taken that the choice of background (see also page 98), or the use of special effects, is not such as to distract listeners – who should be concentrating on your message.

In a spreadsheet data are entered in a table with vertical ruled lines between the columns and horizontal ruled lines between the rows forming a grid – in which the resulting spaces are called cells. Whereas in a printed table, on a page, the number of columns and rows is limited by the type size used and by page size, a spreadsheet can be much larger – according to your needs. You can store data in the cells and by entering appropriate formulae in other cells you can perform calculations, analyse numerical data, and obtain statistics, as with a calculator. Furthermore, data saved on a disk can be edited and if you need to change an entry or add data in extra cells, or even add or delete whole columns or rows of data, recalculations are completed almost immediately and automatically by the computer. You do not have to calculate or recalculate.

Spreadsheets can be used for keeping records of your personal finances, and in business, for example, for recording and analysing sales data, and for accounts. As in word processing, spreadsheets can be printed as hard copy, and if necessary can be incorporated in word-processed documents. Results of the analysis of data, recorded on spreadsheets, can also be used to produce graphs, histograms and charts, and these too can be incorporated in word-processed documents (or in the handouts and visual aids used in presentations).

Practising speaking in a group

If you are apprehensive about standing in front of an audience for the first time, it is probably fear of the unknown, or the thought that you do not know who may be listening. Anyone unused to speaking in a group can gain confidence only with practice. Start by asking questions in lectures and other classes, so that you needn't say much. For example, you might ask for clarification, or for an explanation, or for an example (see page 27). Later you could ask more searching questions, say what you think, or invite others to comment. Then, when you have to lead a discussion or give a talk, start by making a short statement, as a basis for discussion, or by speaking briefly (for no more than two minutes in a meeting, or for as much as five minutes as part of a group presentation).

An interesting exercise, to get people used to speaking with little or no time for preparation (as they have to in an interview or in any conversation or discussion), is to write the name of a suitable subject on a card and to provide a different card, upside down, on the table in front of each member of a group. Each person, in turn, should turn over a card and, after one minute allowed for reflection and for making notes, should speak on the subject for one minute (or, with practice, for longer) with a particular audience in mind. It is easy to speak for up to five minutes, or with experience for fifty minutes, simply by answering the usual six questions (see page 21). For example: *What* is it? *Why* is it useful? *When* is it used? *How* does it work? *Where* can it be purchased? *Who* would find it useful?

In a talk on a subject that interests you, what would you say: (a) to people who share your interest in the subject; (b) to people who have no prior knowledge of the subject; and (c) to people from different backgrounds whose interests you do not know?

Many employers arrange courses to provide appropriate training and practice in public speaking for their managers, and for other employees who may need to address an audience as part of their work; and many colleges organise part-time courses – open to anyone – on such topics as assertiveness, coping with stress, and presentation skills.

Learning from experts

As when learning to play any game, you can improve your own performance by watching experts. When you listen to experienced speakers, consider not only what they say but also how they say it. What do you admire about their performance?

Note also where some speakers go wrong – perhaps from overconfidence rather than a lack of confidence – because they have not followed a few simple rules (see chapter 8, *Speaking to an audience*). Perhaps they have not considered precisely what the people present need to know (see page 73). Perhaps they have used visual aids originally prepared for another talk, instead of planning what they needed to say in this talk and how best to say it (see page 74). Perhaps, because they have not considered the differences between speaking and writing, they pay insufficient attention to their audience – and read a composition that might have been acceptable as a paper in a learned journal but is unacceptable as a talk (see pages 74–6).

Perhaps they have distracting mannerisms that should have been pointed out by a colleague when this or earlier talks were rehearsed (see pages 84–5). However, the most common fault, and the least forgivable because it is the easiest to avoid, is that as a result of inadequate preparation they try to say too much, and so *either* cannot say all they intended to say *or* do not finish on time (see page 106).

Avoiding stress

To avoid stress, always work to an up-to-date job list, so that you tackle tasks in order of priority (see Figure 6.2). Before each day's work starts, list tasks and number them in order of priority. Then delete and add tasks as necessary during the day; and before stopping work up-date your list in preparation for your next day's work.

If you feel nervous about speaking in public, you can gain experience by participating in discussions in seminars and in committees – and making each of your contributions short and to the point.

Nevertheless, you will probably feel apprehensive just before your talk – especially if you are not used to standing in front of an audience. Remember, then, that it is natural to feel keyed up before any important

IMPORTANT URGENT Do first	IMPORTANT LESS URGENT Do second
LESS IMPORTANT URGENT Do third	LESS IMPORTANT LESS URGENT Need not do today

A guide to prioritising tasks

Figure 6.2   Time management. Listing things you need to do will help you to avoid stress – but always use your judgement and remember that less important in this diagram does not mean unimportant.

event, if you are to give a good performance. Like a well-trained athlete before a race, you will gain confidence from knowing that you are well prepared. You are ready to talk to this audience about things you expect them to find of interest.

However, before giving a talk or presentation you might find it helpful to learn and practise relaxation exercises. Many people use them regularly. One method is to sit and allow your skeletal muscles to relax in turn – starting with your toes, your lower leg muscles, your upper legs; your hands, forearms, upper arms, your shoulders, and then the muscles of your face. Alternatively, you may tense your leg, arm and shoulder muscles and then allow them to relax in turn. Such relaxation exercises can be practised at any time – but it is best to use an audio tape that provides expert instruction and advice.

7 Preparing visual aids

One advantage of using a chalkboard, marker-board or flip chart is that you have to prepare effective visual aids quickly at the most appropriate times during your talk. This means that: (a) each visual aid must be clear and simple; (b) you are unlikely to prepare too many; and (c) people have time to observe, think and make notes, as you draw, while you are not speaking.

However, most speakers like to prepare their visual aids in advance, to ensure that the artwork is good and so that they do not have to spend time drawing and writing when they would prefer to be talking. As a result, many speakers use too many visual aids, talk too much, and attempt to present more information than listeners can assimilate in the time available.

Some basic advice

To avoid the most common mistakes in the preparation of visual aids, consider the following advice as if it were a list of rules.

1 Use visual aids as part of your talk, to complement your words, not as ornament. Do not choose them after you have prepared the text of your talk and add them as if they were an afterthought. Instead, when planning each talk, consider how information or ideas can be best conveyed – to the audience you have in mind – in words, numbers, tables or illustrations. If in words, these are best spoken, not written on a visual aid.

2 You may decide to use one visual aid to reinforce each of your main points; and having conveyed information in one way you should not normally repeat it in another way in the same talk.

In this chapter the results presented in a vertical bar chart (Figure 7.1) are also presented in a table (Table 7.1), to illustrate two ways of conveying

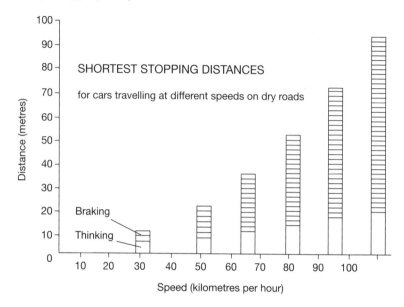

Figure 7.1 A vertical bar chart (also called a column graph). Note: (a) that the
vertical columns do not touch, indicating that the variation in the data
from which the results were obtained is discontinuous (the observations
recorded fall into different groups: in this example, they were records for
cars travelling at the speeds indicated); and (b) that the results presented
in this diagram are the shortest stopping distances for alert drivers,
travelling on dry roads in cars with good tyres and good brakes. Based
on *The Highway Code*, London: HMSO.

the same information. However, when presenting data (observations) or
results (derived by the analysis of data) in a visual aid, having considered
how best to present them to serve your purpose, present them only once.

3 Ensure that the scale on the vertical axis of any graph, histogram or
vertical bar chart starts from zero (as in Figure 7.1). If it does not, the zero
is said to be suppressed. This can make a small difference appear greater
than it actually is, and might be interpreted as a deliberate attempt to
mislead people.

A horizontal bar chart, used for effect in non-technical writing, is
actually a vertical bar chart turned on its side. In this type of diagram the
vertical axis could be labelled 'Years' (as in Figure 7.2) or 'World regions',
for example, and it is the horizontal axis that should normally start from
zero (as in Figure 7.2).

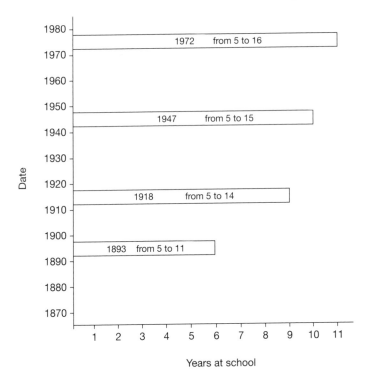

Figure 7.2 Horizontal bar chart: a century of compulsory schooling in Britain (1872 to 1972). Note that by 2003, in England, three-quarters of 17 year olds were either still at school or continuing their education elsewhere (DES, 2005: Table 1).

4 If two diagrams are to be compared ensure that they are drawn to the same scale, and preferably side by side.

5 If you have prepared a sequence of visual aids for one talk do not use the same aids in the same sequence for another, even on the same subject, unless you have checked that they are still up to date, that they are arranged in the right order to support each of your main points, that they still serve your purpose, and that you could not now use other visual aids that would serve your present purpose better.

6 Do not prepare too many visual aids. A talk or presentation is an opportunity for people to see and hear a speaker, to consider what is said, and to ask questions. It should not be just a slide show – unless you are sure that a slide show is what your audience expects. One visual aid to reinforce each of your main points is enough if it is to make an impact at the time and

be remembered. Any unnecessary demonstration, handout or visual aid is a distraction – not an aid.

7 Do not use a visual aid if it includes too many words (see legend to Figure 6.1), or any unnecessary detail or decoration that distracts attention from your message. For visual aids, pictures are better than words. A labelled diagram or drawing, or a cartoon, is effective because it includes a picture as well as words; and for some purposes a picture can be used instead of words (as on many road traffic signs, which make an immediate impact and can be understood even by people who cannot read).

Whereas people can look and listen together, they read at different speeds. Listening unites them, reading sets them apart. So, as a rule, prefer a photograph, a drawing or a diagram to a written message. People have come to see you and hear you talk, not to read words displayed on a screen – and certainly not to hear you read words that you have displayed for them to read.

8 Do not prepare a table that includes too many numbers or has words or numbers that are too small for people to see clearly. Tables and illustrations from books are likely to include more detail than is acceptable in a visual aid, unless they were prepared with both uses in mind. A table in a talk should be a concise summary (results of the analysis of data, not data) to provide your audience with just the information people need to help them appreciate your point (see Table 7.1).

Table 7.1 A table as a visual aid

SHORTEST STOPPING DISTANCES FOR CARS

Speed of car km/h	Thinking distance metres	Stopping distance metres	car lengths
50	10	25	6
80	16	52	13
100	20	92	23

A table used as a visual aid should, preferably, have a title of up to seven words, then up to four vertical columns and up to eight horizontal rows. If you need to provide more information, use a diagram (see Figure 7.1) or a handout, not a table.

9   Use each visual aid to convey a message as clearly and simply as you can, so that it can be understood quickly, but ensure that the information it conveys is accurate and that any statistics are up to date. Ensure that there are no spelling mistakes. Use upper- and lower-case letters, and include only essential punctuation (see Figure 6.1 and Table 7.1). Do not use fancy lettering, elaborate backgrounds or special effects, just because they are available in a computer program. Do not use abbreviations (see page 56).

10   Always make contingency plans so that, if for any reason you are unable to use any audio-visual aids that you have prepared in advance (for example, because of a fault in electrical or electronic equipment), you can talk without them and either have handouts available as an alternative or have chalk and marker pens for use on a chalkboard, on a marker-board or, with a small audience, on a flip chart.

Preparing to use a chalkboard, a marker-board or a flip chart

White or yellow lines and letters show up best on a black or dark green background (as on a chalkboard), and dark blue, dark green, dark red or black on a white background (as with a flip chart, marker-board or screen).

Use capital letters in your notes for any words that may be new to some people in your audience: (a) so that you can write them on a board or flip chart in *large, clear, capital* letters, or display them on a screen; and (b) to remind you to do this, and if necessary, to define them, the first time you use them in your talk.

With a chalkboard or marker-board you can prepare clear, *simple* diagrams quickly, and if necessary you can add to them during your talk (see Figure 7.3) if you have planned them before your talk – so that you are always in control.

A flip chart is useful when talking to a small group. You can arrange key words, definitions and simple diagrams (or blank sheets) in order – before your talk – and then display them as they are required. If you do this, leave a blank sheet after each visual aid – so that people cannot continue to look at your last aid when you have begun to talk about something else and are not yet ready to let them see your next one. Also, if you prepare your charts in advance, you may find it helpful to arrange them in reverse order, so that you can flip each one forward easily during your talk.

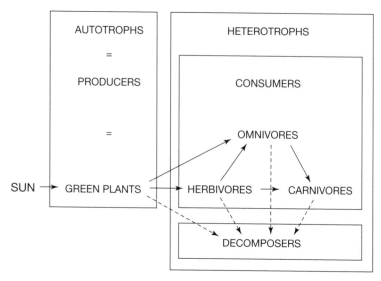

Figure 7.3 Delivery. A simple diagram that could be prepared during a talk or presentation (on a chalkboard, marker-board or overhead projector transparency) by adding a word, a line or an arrow each time you pause briefly to allow your audience time in which to think and make notes.

(a) Having spoken briefly about feeding relationships and energy flow, write the words *sun*, *green plants*, *herbivores* and *carnivores* linked by arrows to represent food consumption and energy flow. At this stage in the talk, the diagram represents a food chain.

(b) Talk about omnivores, introduce the term consumer. Then add the words *omnivores* and *consumers* and three more arrows to the diagram, and draw a rectangle around all the consumers. At this stage in the talk, the diagram represents a food web.

(c) Talk about decomposers and the source of their nutriment. Then add the term *decomposers* and four more arrows to the diagram and draw a rectangle around the word *decomposers*.

(d) Make the distinction between the organisms that use energy from sunlight in photosynthesis (the autotrophs) and organisms that cannot do this (the heterotrophs) which therefore, directly or indirectly, depend on green plants for food. Emphasise this distinction by drawing the two further rectangles on the diagram.

One advantage of preparing visual aids before a talk is that you can check that they can be seen by everyone in the room and that the smallest numbers and letters are easy to read from the back row. However, if you prefer your audience to see how your argument develops or how a diagram is constructed, you may find it helpful to prepare a visual aid (like Figure 7.3) in advance, but in pencil so that (a) you can ensure each diagram is accurate and if necessary to scale; and (b) your audience cannot see the faint words and lines until you go over them with a black broad-tip water-colour marker at appropriate points during your talk.

Preparing to use an overhead projector

As with any other equipment, you will find an overhead projector most useful if you have considered how best to use it.

Check, if possible from the back of the room in which you are to give your talk, that any diagrams and tables you have prepared in advance are clear. Check that you have not included too much detail or anything irrelevant. Whole pages photocopied from books are unsuitable: without enlargement the words (including the labels on illustrations) are likely to be too small to be seen clearly from the back row, as are any numbers.

You are advised to point at the screen, not at the transparency, because you cannot look down at the transparency and up at your audience at the same time. If pointing at the transparency use a fine rod (for example, a narrow-gauge knitting needle). Do not point with your finger, as this would obscure too much of your visual aid.

You may find it helpful to have a suitable card available so that you can deliberately obscure part of a table or diagram – to display just the parts you require at the time. Alternatively, you can build up a diagram (see Figure 7.3) by superimposing transparencies – prepared in advance – at successive stages in your talk.

If you have a separate transparency for each visual aid, place the first one on the projector immediately before you start to speak, so that when you are ready to use it you have only to switch on the light. As with other visual aids, remove each transparency as soon as it has served your purpose.

Always have spare transparencies and suitable pens available so that you can spell any words or prepare simple diagrams or drawings, using the overhead projector instead of a whiteboard or flip chart.

Some overhead projectors have a roll of acetate film on which, for example, you can: (a) write during your talk, and then turn the roll to remove your writing; or (b) prepare a sequence of drawings or diagrams, linked by numbers or arrows, so that you can roll them into view in order, like a flow diagram, to show successive stages in a process. Alternatively, (c) you can fix a transparency below the roll before your talk, to display a drawing, diagram or outline map, so that labelling, symbols or additional artwork can be superimposed by drawing or writing on the roll during the talk – before you turn the roll on so that you can use the same underlay to help you make different points at successive stages in your talk.

Preparing to use a slide projector or a liquid crystal display projector

Relevant photographs add interest to a talk, and a photograph that enables people to see an object or scene is better than a description. So using photographs to illustrate a talk should also save you time.

Photographs serve the double function of depiction and corroboration; but people may be too easily convinced that what they see in a photograph is necessarily correct. A photograph cannot lie but it may mislead. This is especially likely when natural shadows, which give a three-dimensional effect, are destroyed by artificial lighting. In selecting photographs, therefore, look for relevance and interest, sharpness of focus, and effective lighting and contrast, and then consider whether or not a good line drawing or diagram would serve your purpose better. Even if your sole purpose is to entertain, do not include a photograph simply because it is a good one.

To match the interests of your audience, each visual aid should be planned to go with your talk. Remember, as when using a board or flip chart, that white or yellow lines and lettering are best on a black, dark blue or mid-green background, and that black or dark colours are best on a white background. If the slides used in a talk are also to be used in a handout or a publication, prepared with a monochrome printer, then black on a white background is best. The proportions of a table, drawing or diagram for a 5 × 5 cm slide must be 3:4 (see Figures 1.1 and 8.2) or 4:3 (see Figures 6.1, 6.2, 7.1 and 7.3).

Tables that are to be photographed and made into slides can be prepared with a word processor. With appropriate software, these tables can be stored electronically on a disk (see Table 7.1), as can other visual aids (see page 85), and displayed using a liquid crystal display (LCD) projector as an alternative to using slides and a slide projector. However, if you plan to use computer-generated images in a talk, instead of slides, check when you agree to talk that your software is compatible with the hardware and operating system with which it is to be used.

If you are actually using slides (not images stored electronically) arrange them in the same order as in your notes, and check that when projected on to the screen each one is the right way up and the right way round. Sit at the back of a room similar in size to the room in which you will be talking, and check your visual aids for clarity. Do not show a list, diagram or table if it has too many words or numbers – or if any are so small that some people will be unable to read them. If necessary, include blank slides so that your audience does not have to look at a projected image after you have stopped talking about it or before you are ready to talk about it, or at a brilliantly illuminated screen when, before or between slides, no image is projected.

8 Speaking to an audience

On the day of your talk, check that any equipment you need is available, that you know how to use it, and that it is in working order. Check that the light used to illuminate your notes is no brighter than is necessary, and that it will not cause discomfort to anyone in the audience. You should not need to use a microphone unless the acoustics are poor or the room very large, but if you are to use a fixed microphone, ask someone to check your position to ensure that you know either where to stand or how far you can move away from the microphone and still be heard. Then, during your talk, speak only when standing where you know your words will be heard by your audience. Usually you will be next to your notes.

Delivering a talk or presentation

In preparing a talk, most speakers write down exactly what they plan to say and then rehearse to ensure they can complete the talk comfortably in the time available. However, if possible, speak from brief notes (see pages 83–4). Do not read your talk; and do not simply read aloud the words displayed on your visual aids that people can read for themselves.

Before you begin

The impression you make before speaking, as when you meet anyone for the first time, can be based only on the way you present yourself: your appearance, your bearing as you enter the room or rise to speak, your facial expression and your dress (see page 10). As with what you choose to say and how you say it, your appearance should match your subject, your audience and the occasion. Just as you would not talk down to anyone, so you should not dress down for any audience.

To help you to relax, if you feel apprehensive about talking to an audience, you will find it helpful to breathe in deeply and to think of the word *relax* as you breathe out slowly. Do this several times just before starting your talk (see also *Avoiding stress*, page 89). However, confidence comes from being well prepared, knowing exactly what you are going to say and how you will say it: from being in control.

Stand where everyone can see you. When using a chalkboard or other visual aid, stand where you will not obscure anyone's view of the board or screen. When speaking stand next to your notes: this is particularly important if you are using a fixed microphone. If you are not using a microphone, speak loud enough for everyone to hear.

Avoid distracting mannerisms (for example, hand movements that convey no meaning, swinging or banging a pointer, fiddling with equipment, or constantly walking to and fro as if on sentry duty). This is not to say that you should not move your hands: some speakers use carefully considered gestures to good effect.

Start your stop watch

At each stage in your talk you must be sure that you are keeping to time (see page 81). Start your stop watch and place it next to your notes where you can check, when pausing to look at the notes, that you are keeping to time.

Make sure that everyone knows your name

Pause before speaking, as you look around your audience to gain everyone's attention. Then confirm the title of your talk. Make sure everyone knows your name. This is the one occasion when you may repeat information that, at the same time, is displayed on a screen.

Speak so that everyone hears every word

Use the same voice as in normal conversation, the same gestures and the same pauses so that you move forward at the same unhurried pace. But speak more slowly and articulate each word more carefully to ensure that everyone hears every word.

Try not to speak in a monotone: vary the volume and pitch of your voice to emphasise important words and to ensure that the last syllable of each word and the last few words of each sentence are heard. Smile at those times when in conversation you would normally smile; but good advice for most speakers is 'Do not start with a joke' (see *Interest your audience*, page 80). Show your enthusiasm for the subject and your interest in everyone present: look around your audience, using eye contact to capture and maintain attention – so that everyone can see your eyes and your facial expressions and you can see theirs. Remember that audiences are made up of individuals, and speak as if you were talking to a few friends.

Say what you are going to talk about

Give a little more information about the content of your talk than is provided in the title. Remind the audience how what you are about to say relates to their interests and to things they already know. Give the reason for your talk. This is your opportunity, in a few words, to capture attention and promote a desire to listen.

Say when you will answer questions. With a small audience you may encourage questions during your talk but with a large audience this is not practicable.

Maintain the momentum

Get to the point quickly at the start of each aspect of your talk. That is to say, be concise. Do not speak too fast. *Pause briefly* after each main point has been made. The pause (like the paragraph break in a written composition) will help you to emphasise the point, and will let everyone know that it is time to start thinking about the next topic. *Pause also* before talking about each of your visual aids, for long enough for people to study any diagram and read any words themselves. Do not read the words aloud.

Use your notes as reminders

Pause for effect after making each of your main points. Take the opportunity to take a deep breath, to glance at your notes, and to check that you are keeping to time. But always look at your audience when you are speaking. In a talk, audience participation could involve interjections, questions and applause, but in most talks is marked only by eye contact and facial expressions. So, unless your audience is too large, make eye contact with each person from time to time – for just long enough to capture attention – so that all present know you are interested in them and are observing their reactions to your message (see Figure 8.1).

Keep everyone interested

To maintain attention ensure that everyone always has something to do. First, use eye contact to let people know that they have your attention (and that you are expecting some response to your message).

Figure 8.1 Is everybody happy? Maintain eye contact: see how everyone is responding to your message. Who understands? Who looks puzzled, and requires further explanation? Who looks unconvinced, and requires more evidence? Who approves? Who disapproves? Has anyone stopped listening?

You can also ask people to think by using words such as *consider . . . ,* *note . . .* and *observe. . . .* You can ask a question and then pause briefly to give people time to think before answering it yourself in the next part of your talk (or if appropriate by inviting one person, by name, to answer for you). Another way to maintain attention, and help you emphasise an important point, is to provide a change (for example, a specimen, a model, a visual or audio-visual aid or a handout) so that people are not just sitting still, looking at you and listening to the sound of your voice.

Provide handouts only when you need them: not before

If a handout is needed during the talk, do not distribute it until you are ready to speak about it. Then, if you can, hand out enough copies at the end of each row; and walk to the other side of the room to check that everyone has a copy and to collect any spare copies.

Allow time for everyone to become familiar with the layout of the information. Then, after saying what you would like people to note, ask them to put the handout on one side before you continue your talk, saying: 'I shan't be referring to it again' or 'I shall let you know when we need to look at it again.'

If you do not want people to look at a handout during your talk, when it could distract attention from your words, do not distribute it until the end.

Allow people time to study each visual aid

When you write a word on a blackboard or whiteboard, or use some other visual aid to reinforce a main point, there is something for people to see as well as something to hear. Because they can see anything you draw or write during your talk, as you prepare a simple diagram or spell out a word, you may not need to allow them extra time to study such visual aids before you provide any necessary explanation or proceed with your talk.

Otherwise, with visual aids you have prepared in advance, you must give people time to study any diagram or table in silence without the distracting sound of your voice. Then say what you would like them to note and allow time for them to consider your point or to make a note, before you continue with your talk.

If you need to point at the screen, prefer a cane (or a telescopic aerial) to an electronic device. Rest the tip of the pointer for a few seconds on the part to be noted, and then put it down.

Do not display one visual aid when talking about another

If you use a chalkboard or marker-board, keep it clean. If you use a flip chart, turn to a clean sheet as soon as you have made your point. Remove any other visual aid as soon as you have finished with it. Do not allow people to continue looking at things you are no longer talking about, while you are trying to interest them in something else.

Speak only when facing your audience

Maintain eye contact with everyone present. *If you turn away* to draw a diagram or to write a word on a board or chart, *stop talking* immediately. Try not to obscure anyone's view. If you are right-handed stand with the board or overhead projector on your right as you draw or write (with your back to the audience when you use a chalkboard, marker-board or flip chart; but facing your audience at all other times). Take care to make any lines thick enough and any letters large enough to be seen by people sitting at the back of the room.

If possible, when using an overhead projector or slides, use a pointer so that you are not too near the screen. Keep the pointer still, on the detail you want people to note. They will look at the screen when you look at the screen. When you look at your audience you regain everyone's attention and can maintain eye contact as you continue with your talk.

End effectively

If you can bring your talk to an effective conclusion, it should not be nec-essary to say 'In conclusion . . . ' or 'To conclude . . . '. Just summarise each of your main points and state your conclusions clearly. Say, forcefully, why they may be important to your audience. Then sit down – making the end obvious to everyone. Having thanked the organisers at the beginning for asking you to speak, do not say 'Thank you' again at the end merely to indicate, weakly, that you have now finished! Your last words should be important words that you would like everyone to remember.

Ask questions

If the purpose of your talk is to give instruction, it is important that you should ask questions to check that everyone has understood and can remember essential points.

With a small audience this can be done at a suitable point during your talk and again at the end.

Answer questions

In a short presentation or with a large audience, questions are best left until the end. Questions from the audience, and your answers, may add relevant information or ideas, or help to prevent misunderstandings. In preparing your talk you will have noted likely questions (see page 82) and will have notes of any examples or statistics needed for a satisfactory answer.

People ask questions for different reasons. Most ask to obtain additional information or for clarification. Remain at the front of the room facing your audience. Make a note of each question, as it is being asked. Then repeat the question, (a) to confirm that you heard and understood what the questioner would like to know; (b) to ensure that everyone in the audience understands; and (c) to allow yourself a few seconds for thought while composing your answer. Then keep your answer brief, clear and to the point.

The most thought-provoking questions are likely to be those you have not anticipated. If you are interested in the subject and well prepared you will probably be able to answer them. However, if asked a question that you cannot answer, do not attempt an answer. One way to deal with such a question is to ask if anyone in the audience knows the answer. Another way is to take the name of the questioner and say you will get in touch when you have had time to find the answer. There is a limit to what anyone knows on any subject: any child can soon take an expert to the frontiers of knowledge simply by asking the question 'Why?'

Some who speak during the question time may simply wish to express interest, to provide an example in support of your argument, or to express a different point of view. As they have not asked a question, it may be sufficient for you to thank each of them for the contribution.

If there are no questions, you can use the time remaining to answer some of the questions you had anticipated might be asked, or to provide bibliographic details of sources of further information (perhaps as a handout, see pages 79 and 121–3).

Finish on time

Nobody will mind if your talk ends a few minutes early but you must not speak for too long. If you were allowed to start on time, it is up to you to time each stage in your talk so that you say all that you need to say, in the way you have planned to say it, and finish on time – while everyone is still interested and listening attentively. Leave people to reflect on your words. If you talk for too long they will soon stop listening, become exasperated, and may remember only that you did not know when to stop.

Leading a discussion

Participating in discussions, as part of a course on communication skills, contributes to the development of other interpersonal skills as well one's listening and speaking skills. It should therefore enable students to benefit more from tutorials and seminars; and to organise, participate in and lead meetings of self-help groups. The experience of working in and leading discussions will also help them later, in any career based on their studies.

Discussion groups are most useful when people with different interests, experience and expertise are brought together to consider a matter of common interest (for example, a problem, procedure or practice) and so increase their understanding (as in a training session) or to work on a clearly defined task, make a decision or list recommendations.

Be prepared

For each discussion it is best to sit at small tables, with enough space for note-making, and with the tables arranged so that participants can see one another and have a clear view of the flip chart, board or overhead projector screen used by the discussion leader – who also needs a table and access to the other tables (for example, to distribute handouts at appropriate points in the discussion).

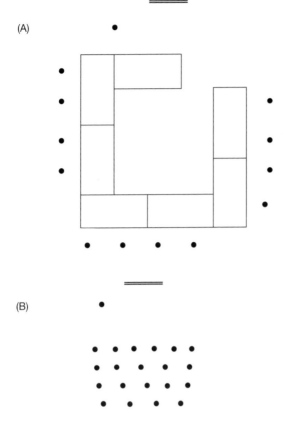

Figure 8.2 Seating arrangements: (A) for a small discussion group or workshop, with up to twelve participants, requiring a marker-board, a flip chart or a screen, and with the discussion leader or instructor free to move close to each of the other participants when necessary; and (B) for a more formal presentation to a larger group.

Twelve people are enough for a good discussion (see Figure 8.2A). With more than twelve it may be difficult for everyone to contribute; and it may also be necessary to accept less satisfactory seating arrangements (see Figure 8.2B).

In contrast to a talk or lecture when one speaker is conveying information or ideas, or trying to persuade, the role of a discussion leader (as in a seminar) is: (a) to provide a brief introduction; (b) to encourage everyone present to contribute; (c) to listen; and then (d) to question; (e) to ask for evidence or clarification when necessary; (f) to summarise the discussion at intervals – so that, in the time available, from the points of view expressed, it is possible to come to a conclusion or end with a list of possibilities.

It follows that to lead a discussion you must know your subject and be aware of the interests of the participants. As with a written composition, you need a title or heading to give a purpose and direction to the work. This could be a question, 'How should we . . . ?', or it could be the statement of an objective, 'To improve our understanding of . . . '.

Then list relevant topics, arrange them in an appropriate order as a discussion outline, and make a note of questions you could ask to stimulate the discussion of each topic. Your list of topics could also be displayed on a chart, before the discussion starts, and referred to in your introduction. But your task is to listen and guide, not to dictate the proceedings, so after your introduction you should be open to suggestions as to additional topics, as to the relative importance of topics, and as to the order in which the topics should be considered. Alternatively, you could *either* (a) start with a heading on a flip chart, list the participants' suggestions as to topics that should be considered, and then agree on an appropriate order; *or* (b) start with just a heading and a concise introduction, and then give participants time to think for themselves, and to work together in smaller groups before they all agree on a list of relevant topics and arrange them in an appropriate order (for example, see *Prepare a set of instructions*, page 109).

Question

Usually, your discussion outline will give you an idea of how much time you can allow for a consideration of each topic. You may start the discussion with a question relevant to the first topic. Then you must allow time for serious thought. Do not be tempted to provide an answer yourself. Each time you ask a question, use silence to provoke others to speak. People considering the question will not all be ready to answer at once. A minute may seem a long time for you to await an answer, but it will also seem a long time to others if you remain silent. It will give everyone time to think; then someone will speak.

Make a note of each contribution: one word may be enough to remind you. If you don't speak, someone else is likely to do so. If no one speaks you could ask: 'Who would like to suggest . . . ?' Then, if necessary, you could ask someone directly: 'What do you think of that idea?' or 'How would that fit in with . . . ?'

By asking open questions (most of which begin with the words *what*, *why*, *when*, *how*, *where* or *who* (see Table 2.2), you can avoid closed questions (discussion-stopping) to which the answer is 'Yes' or 'No'. It is also important, early in a discussion, to avoid leading questions such as 'Do you agree that . . . ?' or 'Don't you think that . . . ?', which hint at an acceptable answer; but at the end of a discussion, when summing up, you might well say 'We are agreed that . . .'.

By asking for clarification, for evidence or for examples, you can maintain everyone's attention, promote further thought, invite contributions to the discussion, check that an individual understands, and help ensure that all understand. By asking for a description or explanation when necessary, you can help ensure that everyone understands the relevance of a contribution.

It can be helpful if someone known to have a special interest in any subject being discussed (for example, a tutor) does not speak until all other participants have had the opportunity to express their thoughts on each topic. Otherwise, some may be inclined to bow to authority – instead of providing a fresh approach to a topic about which they have not previously given much thought. Different views should also be sought by giving all present the opportunity to express their thoughts on each topic, without trying to make anyone speak who prefers to remain silent.

Summarise

Noting the gist of each contribution during the discussion will help you to summarise the facts stated, people's feelings or the opinions expressed, when you feel enough time has been devoted to a topic. Your summary, with notes added as sub-headings below the topic heading on a flip chart, should also help you to move on to the next topic, and to a new question that promotes further discussion.

Your own notes will also enable you, at the end of the discussion, to summarise both: (a) the main points raised under each heading; and (b) the group's answer to the question posed at the beginning or, for example, courses of action considered practicable or conclusions reached.

Everyone present should benefit from a discussion, including the discussion leader, and reflect on what has been learned. And anyone who organises discussions on one topic with different groups of people should learn something from each group.

Improve your performance

Prepare a set of instructions

We all use instructions: what to do in the event of fire; how to change the batteries in a radio; how to hard-boil an egg (see Figure 6.1). Whenever we ask anyone to do anything, unless we know that they already have enough experience of the task to complete it satisfactorily, we must give good instructions.

A discussion topic that will interest any group can begin with the instruction: 'Write a set of instructions headed "How to write a set of instructions"'. After introducing this task, an effective way to organise this discussion (lasting about an hour) is to allow participants to think for about ten minutes with no one speaking, as they list points to be included in the instructions, and then ask them to discuss their lists in pairs for a further ten minutes. This is one way of ensuring that all present do feel that they have contributed to the discussion. All can then benefit from sharing ideas in groups of four, for perhaps another ten minutes. The discussion leader can then list (on a board, flip chart or overhead projector transparency) participants' suggestions as to points that should be included. Then everyone can participate in the discussion. How should each instruction be expressed? In what order should the instructions be listed?

Questions that could be used to promote further discussion include: Why are some of the sets of instructions you are asked to follow better than others? Why do you find some confusing or annoying? Who should be involved in preparing instructions for a particular task? When should written instructions be provided? How should written instructions be set out? To whom should they be issued, or where should they be displayed? What is the only acceptable test for a set of instructions?

In about twenty minutes some agreement will be possible as to what is necessary in a set of instructions, but participants will appreciate that with further thought they could improve their lists. This is the purpose of any discussion: to stimulate thought, to promote the sharing of information and ideas, and to increase understanding.

What do you expect of a set of instructions? Do the instructions in Figure 6.1 satisfy your requirements? How can you decide whether or not this is a good set of instructions?

Later, perhaps at the next meeting of the discussion group, participants could consider the suggestions in Table 8.1, which are based on discussions involving many groups of people – with different interests but with the same discussion leader.

Assess your own performance

After giving a talk or leading a discussion, consider how others reacted (how they looked and what they said) and your own feelings. Reflect. What went well? Was everyone attentive throughout? What interested people most? Did you fit each topic (in your topic outline for the talk or in your discussion outline for the discussion), comfortably, into the time you had allocated for it? Did you attempt to achieve too much in the time available? Was there anything that did not work as well as you had expected? Were there any questions that you had not anticipated? It is good practice to record your answers to such questions in a reflective log (see page 43).

What have you learned that will help you to do better next time? But remember, if you do have to speak on the same subject again, that it is unlikely to be appropriate to simply attempt a repeat performance. A different audience is likely to have different expectations and needs. You may consider different aspects of the subject and choose different examples. There may be recent developments that you should mention. For one audience your intention may be to instruct or inform, for another to convince or persuade, for another to entertain or provoke. Therefore, prepare each talk or discussion for a particular audience (in four stages, see Table 3.1), so that what you say is well suited to the occasion.

Feedback forms

At the end of many lecture courses in universities and colleges students are asked to complete an assessment form relating to the course content and its delivery.

A lecturer who hands out feedback forms in the last of a series of lectures may also collect them, analyse them and consider both the results of this analysis and the comments of individuals. That is to say, to encourage constructive person-to-person feedback, the forms may be seen only by this lecturer and used in a critical assessment of the success of this part of the course and in an attempt by the lecturer to maintain or improve his or her own performance and so the quality of the course as a whole.

Alternatively, feedback forms may be handed out, collected and analysed by the course tutor (or by some other administrator), not by the lecturer or lecturers who delivered the course – who may then see only the results of the analysis of the data the students provided.

If students are instructed not to sign the forms, or add anything that could indicate their identity, they should not take the opportunity under the shelter of this anonymity to indicate their disapproval of a lecturer resulting, for example, from their having obtained lower marks than they had expected for course work assessed by this lecturer.

Students completing these forms should bear in mind that they have benefited from improvements in the course content and delivery following feedback from both academic staff and students in previous years. Anything they write will be considered by either the lecturer concerned or by the board of studies responsible for the course, or both, when with the benefit of further experience they seek to maintain or where possible improve the quality of the course for the next year's students. All that is required of students, therefore, is an honest, carefully considered answer to each question on the feedback form (such as they might expect themselves had they given the course).

The set work students hand in for marking is another source of feedback to lecturers: (a) about their own performance; and (b) about their students' ability to understand the work and to integrate information from their class work with that obtained from other sources.

Table 8.1 How to prepare a set of instructions[a]

Stages	Instructions[b]		Essentials
THINK			
	1	Consider who may use the instructions, and how they will be used.	**Consideration for the user**
	2	Ensure you can complete the task well yourself.	**Knowledge, understanding**
	3	Precede the instructions with any necessary explanation, words of caution, warning or possible danger[c]	Safety
	4	Give the instructions a concise but informative heading (as above).	
	5	List any materials or equipment required.	
	6	Break the task into steps: the things to be done, explaining the action required, at each step.	**Explanation**[d]
PLAN			
	7	Arrange the steps in order of performance, so that completing the last step completes the task.	**Order**
	8	Include any photographs, drawings or diagrams, intended to help the user, next to the instructions they illustrate.	**Appropriateness**
WRITE			
	9	Write in the imperative (with each step one instruction or command), as in this list.[e]	
	10	Make each instruction as simple as possible.	**Simplicity**
	11	Write each instruction as a complete sentence, using words users will not misunderstand, to ensure it is unambiguous.	**Clarity**
	12	State any safety precautions immediately before any step at which special care is needed, preceded by the word **CAUTION**, the word **DANGER** or the word **WARNING**, as appropriate.[c]	Safety
	13	Number the steps, to draw attention to the action required at each step.	

Table 8.1 continued

Stages	Instructions[b]	Essentials
	14 State any observations, to be made at each step, that indicate a satisfactory outcome.	
	15 Express each quantity mentioned as a number and an SI unit of measurement, unless other units are marked on the equipment to be used.	**Precision**
CHECK		
	16 Undertake the task, following your instructions, to check that they are accurate, in order of performance, and complete.	**Accuracy** **Completeness**
	17 **REVISE** the instructions, if necessary.	
	18 Ask someone else, with experience of the task, to undertake the task, following the instructions, and to suggest any improvements.	**Coherence**
	19 **REVISE** the instructions, if necessary.	
	20 Ask at least one other person, with appropriate experience, but who has not previously performed the task, to undertake the task following your instructions, and to suggest any improvements.	
	21 **REVISE** the instructions if necessary.	
	22 End instructions for use within an organisation, if appropriate, with a statement indicating to whom users should send comments or suggestions. For example: 'Let me know if you encounter any difficulties or have any suggestions for improving either the procedure or these instructions'.	
	23 Sign and date the instructions. In doing this you take responsibility for them. As with any other communication, do not sign unless you have the authority to do so.	

Notes

a   Based on Barrass *Writing at Work: a Guide to Better Writing in Administration, Business and Management* (2002).

b   Anyone writing safety precautions, user guides, operating instructions, technical manuals, protocols, procedures or similar documents, containing instructions, must ensure that they conform to relevant Standards. They must also satisfy themselves that their responsibilities to users under product liability and health and safety legislation have been met. For example, see DTI (1988) *Instructions for Consumer Products* (London: HMSO) and the ISO/IEC Guide 37:1995 *Instructions for Use of Products of Consumer Interest*.

c   The word *caution* draws attention to a low risk (of damage to the product, process or surroundings), the word *warning* to a medium risk, and the word *danger* to a high risk (of injury or death).

d   Words printed in bold in this table, as being essential in good instructions, are also essential in all scholarly communications.

e   Most instructions begin with a verb to indicate immediately the action required, but if an observation or decision has to be made before the action is taken the sentence may start with 'If' or 'When'.

9 Finding information

We learn many things by personal observation, using our five senses, and constantly relate new observations to our previous experience. Most of our conversation is based on this store of knowledge. Also, if we cannot remember something or need to know more about any topic, we can usually refer to our notes or ask someone else – perhaps another student or a lecturer – to advise, explain or help. This chapter is about finding and using other sources of information.

Sources of information

Information technology is concerned with electronic methods of cataloguing, communicating, processing, storing, retrieving and publishing information. People speak of the electronic office as a place where there is no need for paper, and it is often convenient to use computer-based information retrieval systems to locate answers to our questions, but remember: (a) that much information is still recorded, stored and communicated on paper; and (b) that much of the information available in the teaching rooms and libraries of colleges and universities (like the papers available to other people working in other places) is likely to be well suited to your immediate needs – and unavailable elsewhere.

Dictionaries

A dictionary of the English language is an essential reference book for any student (see page 54). For anyone who needs more information than can be included in a desk dictionary, the *Oxford English Dictionary* is a printed multi-volume work that is also available in CD-ROM and in an online version that provides access from a computer terminal to a database comprising more than 500,000 words.

There are also dictionaries of the specialist or technical terms of most subjects, and there are dictionaries of abbreviations, but these may not be up to date – and they may be incomplete or otherwise inaccurate. Such reference books are no substitute for good textbooks, on each of your subjects, in which essential terms and abbreviations should be explained when they are introduced and then used in appropriate contexts.

Encyclopaedias

An encyclopaedia is a good starting point for anyone coming new to a subject. Well-known general encyclopaedias include the single-volume *Hutchinson's Encyclopaedia*, the multi-volume *Encyclopaedia Britannica* (also available as a multimedia version on CD-ROM) and the multimedia *Encarta* (on CD-ROM). In addition to such general works there are specialist encyclopaedias on many subjects.

The entries in a printed encyclopaedia are in alphabetical order. Each entry is a concise article, by an acknowledged authority, and it ends with references to other sources of further information for those who need to know more. Also, if you look up key words in the index of a printed encyclopaedia you may find other articles of immediate interest – as you may by entering key words in computer-aided information retrieval. Multimedia publications provide spoken words and other sounds as well as printed text, and moving pictures as well as stills.

Handbooks

There are concise reference books for day-to-day use on most subjects. For example, Gowers's *The Complete Plain Words* (1986) is a handbook for all those who use words as tools of their trade.

Other handbooks, usually called technical manuals, are supplied with many commercial products. Each manual describes a product and provides instructions, as appropriate, on how to store, handle, install, use, maintain and service it correctly, and when the time comes dispose of it safely.

Standards

Many national and international organisations produce standards to encourage uniformity in, for example, the use of units of measurement and the content, layout, preparation and management of documents.

The following are examples of American (ANSI), British (BS) and International (ISO) standards available in printed and CD-ROM versions (and also via the Internet): *International System of Units (SI units)* BS 5555 (or ISO 1000); *References to published materials* (including bibliographic and cartographic materials, computer software and databases) BS 1629 (similar to ISO 690); *Scientific papers for written and oral presentation: preparation* ANSI Z39.16; *Statistics, vocabulary and symbols* BS ISO 3534.

Directories

There are directories covering many subjects – including companies, trades and other organisations. Names and addresses may be included, as in a telephone directory, and other information. Many directories are available in printed and electronic versions. For example, all the names and telephone numbers in a complete set of the United Kingdom *Phone Book* are also available online (and, as stand-alone or multi-user versions, on CD-ROM). Access to other constantly up-dated computer-based sources of information is also available via television and via the Internet.

Books

It is not possible to keep all the books on one subject together on the shelves of a library. To find out which books on any subject are stocked by a library, first look for the classification number for that subject in the subject index. Then look up this number in the subject catalogue, where you should find an entry for each book stocked. The book number in each entry indicates where the book with this number is to be found on the shelves.

If you know which book you require use the alphabetical catalogue, in which the names of authors or editors (and those of organisations, government departments and societies that produce books) are listed in alphabetical order. Each entry in this catalogue includes bibliographic details of a book (or of another source of information) and its classification number.

In some libraries each entry in the classified and alphabetical catalogues is on a separate index card or on microfiche, but in most libraries access to the main catalogues is via a computer keyboard. Detailed instructions on how to use the catalogues are displayed on the computer screen. You can search: (1) by entering a classification number to see what books the library stocks on a particular subject; or (2) by entering the name of an author, the name of an organisation or, if you are looking for a particular book, the title of a book; or (3) by entering a key word that you think is likely to be included in the title of a book on the subject that is of interest to you. By entering a key word you may also find details of relevant non-book materials available in the library (for example, maps, collections of photographs, audio and video tapes, and public records on microfilm). However, remember that a key word search will help you find only those entries that have the key words you chose in their titles (see below), whereas a subject search should provide you with a list of all titles on the subject that are stocked by the library.

Reviews

Some books and journals specialise in the publication of articles reviewing the literature on a particular subject, and some reviews are published in journals that also publish original papers. In a review all relevant published work should be considered, so a review is a good starting point in a literature survey. However, reviews may say nothing of the methods used in the work reviewed and each reference to previous work is necessarily brief and may be misleading. Because books and reviews contain material from earlier publications they are called secondary sources. You must look at original articles (primary sources) to be sure that in speaking or writing about the work of others you do not misrepresent them.

Specialist journals

The results of original research are published in specialist journals. In these primary sources you can read the results of recent work soon after it is published and see references to related articles that may be of interest.

It is not possible for any library to subscribe to all journals, but many are published in electronic as well as print versions, and some only in electronic versions; computer-based information retrieval systems provide easy access to the titles and abstracts of articles in both current issues and back numbers of most of them.

A search for articles on a particular subject can be based on key words (words that you would expect to be included in the titles of articles or in journal indices). You can also refine your search by using the operators *and*, *or* and *not*. But note that care is needed when using these operators. If you enter *birds and nests* you will find only articles containing both these key words; if you enter *birds or nests* you will find references in the publications searched to either birds or nests separately and to both birds and nests; and if you enter *birds not nests* you will find only those in which birds are mentioned, not those in which both birds and nests are mentioned.

The Internet

With a web browser, you can use the web address of a business or other organisation to access its website from a personal computer and see the pages it provides – which include, for example, words, pictures, videos, plans and maps. Via the Internet, therefore, much useful information is available – but also much unsupported opinion and much that is fiction.

Unlike the papers published in professional journals (in printed or electronic versions), much of the material on web pages has not been subject to peer review and editing. Also, the contents of web pages may be changed at any time, so it may not be possible to state the source of information obtained from web pages in such a way that readers can consult the same source and read an identical document themselves. Keep these reservations in mind when you use the Internet. Also, because web pages may change at any time, if a document is of particular interest you are advised to download it to your computer or to make a hard copy.

Many organisations include a web address on their headed notepaper and in advertisements, and there are directories of web addresses, but if you do not know an address you can try to guess it: most web addresses comprise: www (the World Wide Web), the name of the organisation (for example ons = Office of National Statistics), an extension indicating the type of organisation (for example com = company; gov = government), and the country (for example UK = United Kingdom) – with full stops where there are commas in this sentence but with no spaces. For example, www.ons.gov.uk is the web address of the Office of National Statistics, a government department in the United Kingdom. Web addresses can also be located using search engines of an Internet Service Provider (ISP): for example, Google at http://www.google.com. However, when you access a web address you must check that the site is that of the organisation you are seeking – because different organisations, perhaps with opposing objectives, may have very similar addresses.

Via the Internet you can also, for example: (a) study previously inaccessible archives; (b) browse through the catalogues of major libraries; (c) scan pages of both current issues and back numbers of newspapers; (d) search indices for bibliographic details and abstracts of publications likely to be of interest to you (see Table 9.1); and (e) read articles from journals published electronically (which, if necessary, you can print out or download to your computer).

Literature Online (LION) is an electronic database of works of English and American literature that can be searched, for example, by author, title or key word. And if you need to know whether or not a book you require is in print, or whether or not a copy you have is the latest edition, you can

Table 9.1 Some electronic sources of information on articles published in journals

Electronic sources[a]	Access to[b]
America: History and Life	Books, reviews, media and journals
Analytical Abstracts	Chemistry and analytical chemistry
Art Abstracts	Art, history of art, museums, photography, films
Biosis	Biology, medicine, veterinary science
EBSCO	Business, marketing, management and
Business Sources Elite	economics journals
FT McCarthy	Company, industry and market information
Geobase	Earth science, geology, geography, marine science
Historical Abstracts	World history (excluding USA and Canada)
INSPEC	Computing, electrical and electronic engineering, information technology
pubMed	Medicine, life sciences, psychology
Philosopher's Index	Books and journals on philosophy
PsycINFO	Psychology and related subjects
Sociological Abstracts	Abstracts of articles from sociology journals
Web of Knowledge	Science Citation Index, Social Science Citation Index and Arts & Humanities Citation Index
Zetoc	Tables of contents of journals and conference proceedings in the British Library

Notes
a   As with other businesses and organisations, the names, ownership and location of electronic sources may change.
b   Libraries with access to computerised indices provide notes to help users.

find full bibliographic details of any book that is in print via the Internet by entering the author's name (for example, via Copak at http://www.ac.uk) which provides access to the merged online catalogues of major research libraries in the UK and Ireland plus those of both the British Library and the National Library of Scotland; or via WorldCat, which may be accessed either direct (at http://www.oclc.org/worldcat/open/default.htm) or via Google.

The Internet also makes available online instruction. For example, many of the course materials produced by the Open University in England are available via the Internet, with tutorial support, to students in many countries in Western Europe.

Many people have Internet accounts with an Internet Service Provider and pay for this either by a direct charge or through a telephone company. Anyone making much use of a personal computer will find use of the

Internet expensive, because a search for information can take a long time. You pay directly because of the cost of the service, and indirectly if you value your time. Also: (a) your search will not necessarily be successful; and (b) you will not be able to rely on the relevant material you do find, much of which is likely to be opinion – unsupported by evidence. As when reading review articles (secondary sources), you will need to refer to primary sources (see page 117) for the evidence upon which any statements are based.

Many of the search engines used in looking for information on the Internet offer both a simple search and a more complex search that may be called an advanced search. However, no search engine could search the whole of the Internet, and if you enter identical search requests into different search engines you will find differences in their outputs even when searching for specialist terms. One reason for these differences is that organisations developing web pages use many different key words, not just the most appropriate words, in an attempt to direct searches to their pages. Another reason is that some search engines accept new web pages quicker than others, and some store pages for longer than others.

Intranets

An intranet is a web, similar to the Internet, but with restricted access. For example, it may be available within a college or university, linking computers on the same site or on different sites. Within an international company it may link computers on sites in different countries. Because access is restricted the information available in an intranet is easier to control and is likely to be of better quality than much of the information available on the Internet. If you are in an organisation that has an intranet, therefore, this should be where you concentrate your first online searches.

Other sources of information available in libraries

Visual aids, including maps, photographs, tapes and slides, compact disks and videos, may be kept in a separate visual aids section, or with books on the shelves; or they may be available in map rooms or other rooms as part of special collections. If the library's catalogues are computer based, any non-book materials available in the library will probably be included on the database. Also, ask a librarian if you would like to know about the open learning and computer-based learning materials you can access from a computer terminal in the library.

Improve your performance

Read to some purpose

When you are preparing a talk or presentation you may read to get background information or to find answers to specific questions. You read in search of facts but much of what you read may not be factual. As in studying your subjects, you must always read critically – to distinguish evidence from opinion, and impartial from prejudiced comment.

If searching for the current position on any subject, try to obtain the most recent edition of any book to which you refer. You may find reference books most convenient, but remember that other books, written to be read as a whole, can also be read in part. From key words in the index or list of contents you should be able to find the pages, paragraphs or sentences relevant to your immediate needs.

Make notes as you read

Having decided what to read it is essential to record, accurately, complete bibliographic details of the publication either on an index card or, preferably, at the top of a sheet of paper on which you can make notes and, later, interleave with your other notes on the subject – so that for each subject you have only one set of notes.

You need complete bibliographic details of each source of information from which you make notes, so that: (a) you can remember the source of the notes; (b) you can refer to the same source again at any time; (c) you have all the information to hand if you decide to include details of this source in a handout or visual aid – or in a list of references at the end of a written assignment; and (d) you can obtain any other publication cited in this source. See Table 9.2 for advice as to the information required when recording bibliographic details of a book; and see Table 9.3 for similar advice relating to a journal, magazine or newspaper article.

In the bibliographic details of a chapter in a book, the writer's name comes first, then the date of publication of the book, then the chapter heading, which should not be underlined or printed in italics, followed by the word *in* (underlined in handwriting or printed in italics) and this by a colon, the name(s) of the editor(s), the abbreviation ed. or eds, the other details as for a book, and then the first and last pages of the chapter.

When recording the source of information from an Internet site, note the name of the originator (author, editor or organisation), the date and title (as for a book, see Table 9.2), followed by the word [online] in square brackets, the place of publication, the publisher (if known), the word

Table 9.2 How to record complete bibliographic details of a book

---

Author's or editor's surname and initials (or name of issuing organisation if no author or editor is named).

Year of publication in parenthesis (here or later, see below, depending on house rules).

Title of book, underlined in handwriting or typescript and printed in italics, with initial capitals used for most words.

The edition number (except for the first edition).

The number of volumes (e.g. 2 vols) or the volume number (in arabic numerals, underlined with a wavy line in handwriting and printed in bold) but without the abbreviation vol.

The place of publication followed by the name of the publisher, or vice versa, and the year of publication if this has not already been included.

Either the number of the page (p.) or pages (pp. –) referred to or the number of pages in the book (pp.) including preliminary pages (those before page 1).

Note
For examples, see Bibliography (page 133).

Table 9.3 How to record complete bibliographic details of an article in a journal, magazine or newspaper

---

Author's surname and initials.

Year of publication in parenthesis.

Title of paper, which should not be underlined or printed in italics, with capitals used only for words that would require them in any sentence.

The name of publication (underlined in handwriting or typescript and printed in italics, like the names of all publications).

The volume number (underlined with a wavy line in handwriting and printed in bold) without the abbreviation vol.

The issue number (in parenthesis) or the date of issue.

The first and last pages of the article, joined by a dash.

Example
Horowitz, R. B. and Barchilon, M. G. (1994) Stylistic guidelines for e-mail, *IEEE Transactions on Professional Communication*, 37 (4) 207–212.

Available, and then the name of the service provider, an Internet address, and [the date accessed] in square brackets.

When recording bibliographic details of a book or of an article published in a journal which is also available on the Internet, include the usual reference details (see Tables 9.2 and 9.3) followed by the medium (for example, online) and then by details of the Internet site.

Always record the date on which you make any further notes, the name of the library from which you obtained the publication, and the page number from which you make each note, so that you can find the page again if necessary, or refer to it in citing the source of your information.

Your notes will usually be brief (key words and phrases, headings and sub-headings, concise summaries and simple diagrams) but take care that they are accurate. Such brief notes will be useful in filling gaps in your topic outline for a talk or for a written assignment.

In summarising make a clear distinction in your notes between the author's conclusions and your own comments, so that you do not misrepresent the author's views later. Do not waste time copying out long passages word for word. If you think you may need to quote from a publication it is best to make a photocopy, but if this is not practicable make sure you write every word and punctuation mark exactly as on the page from which you are copying, plus quotation marks to remind you that it is a quotation. This ensures that later you cannot inadvertently include other people's thoughts in your own work without proper acknowledgement of their source.

To copy complete sentences from a composition written by someone else and present them as your own, that is to say without acknowledging their source, would be plagiarism (stealing thoughts) and this is unacceptable – whether you are writing or speaking.

As a student, you are advised to integrate your notes from publications with those made in conversations (see page 24), in lectures, tutorials and seminars (see page 31) and when reflecting on your work in private study – so that you have only one set of notes on each aspect of your work.

Cite sources of information

Do not cite a source of information in any talk or presentation, or in anything you write, unless you have read it – as a whole or in part – to check that you are not misrepresenting the author.

If you use an author's exact words, say whose words you are quoting and, if necessary, display the words and punctuation marks (between quotation marks) in a visual aid. You may also provide a handout listing complete bibliographic details of all the sources mentioned in your talk.

If you summarise information or ideas from compositions written by other people, instead of using their exact words, you should still acknowledge their source: (a) to acknowledge the work of others; (b) so that listeners know that the views expressed are not necessarily your own; and (c) so that they can look at the same publications themselves.

10 Speaking in an interview

Interviews are arranged for many purposes. This chapter is about: (a) selection interviews, as for a college or university course, for vacation employment or for a permanent post; (b) oral examinations, in which a student is questioned by an external examiner; and (c) counselling interviews, in which a student seeks help by discussing some personal problem affecting his or her ability to study but not directly connected with the subjects being studied.

Selection interviews

Each selection interview is an unrepeatable opportunity to speak for yourself. Before applying for a place at college or university, for vacation employment or for a permanent post, find out as much as you can about the course or about the employer. This research is important: it should increase your chances of success in obtaining an interview, and affect your approach to the interview, your ability to judge whether or not the course or the work is right for you, and so perhaps the rest of your life. The more you know about a course or about an employer before an interview, the better you will be able to talk about the work that will be expected of you. You should be ready to ask sensible questions.

Choosing a college or university course

You probably studied a variety of subjects at school, as part of a broad education, and then selected certain subjects to take in examinations. Studying these subjects may have helped you to decide what to do next. More than this, it provided a foundation for your further studies. You might have encountered difficulties if after studying these subjects you had decided to change direction – to study different subjects at college or university or to make a career in work normally based on the study of other subjects.

These things are true at each stage in your formal education. If you plan to specialise in a particular subject in your later years at college or university, you may have to study this subject and others (called prerequisites) in the earlier years. On the other hand, if you are not sure which is to be your main subject, you should try to take a choice of subjects in your first year that will enable you to decide, later, to specialise in one or two of them.

Consider what kind of course you should take and then find out what courses of this kind are available. You can do this by writing to the colleges or universities at which you think you might like to study. Read the information they supply. Make such enquiries as far in advance of your preferred starting date as possible, so that you can complete your applications and submit them before any closing dates.

The entry requirements for an advanced course are such that, having satisfied them, you should be able to cope with the more advanced work. However, before starting any course of study, try to assess your suitability for the course and for the kind of career likely to follow from such studies. If you have a particular career in mind, talk to people who already have the qualification at which you are aiming. Question them about their work and about career prospects. Consider their advice. Also, look at the booklets on careers published, for example, by different professional bodies and institutes.

Applying for vacation employment or for a permanent post

When applying for employment you may approach an employer by sending a *curriculum vitae* (*résumé*) and a covering letter in which you state your interest in the employer and draw particular attention to relevant qualifications (which you will also have emphasised in your *curriculum vitae*). Alternatively, you may respond to an advertisement by requesting further particulars and an application form.

A good advertisement provides the information needed to attract the attention of suitably qualified readers and to encourage them to apply. Then the further particulars sent to applicants with the application form should include a job description: a statement of the education, experience and training required, of any equipment to be used and operations to be performed, and of the opportunities and responsibilities involved, to make clear how the person appointed is expected to fit into the organisation.

Before an interview for employment, as when applying for a college or university place, there is always enough time for preparation. Read the further details sent with the application form and find out as much as you can about the employer from other sources (for example, from the organisation's annual report or website, from directories available in libraries, from products advertised and on sale, and if possible from current employees). The more you know about the post advertised, the employer, and the selection procedures used, the better you will be placed to ask sensible questions and talk about the work that will be expected of you.

Before any formal interview, if you are given a guided tour of the accommodation or shown equipment, you may be asked questions – and have the opportunity to ask questions and display your interest – and so to create a good first impression. Learn as much as you can from your conversations and observations. Bear in mind that the person taking you round may be present at your interview, or may be asked for comments on each applicant prior to the interview.

Before and during the interview, you will be thinking: Is this work I could do well? Would I find it satisfying? How would I fit in? What would be the challenges, opportunities and prospects for me in this employment?

Being interviewed

The people interviewing you, for an advanced course or for employment, must decide – in a short time – how interested you are, how enthusiastic, and how well qualified. They also make judgements about your personality.

The interview for a course of study will probably be informal. Your visit to the college or university is as much to help you to make sure that you choose the right course as to help the college or university to select the right students. Your interview is an opportunity to discuss your interests and the course content, and to ask questions. You should expect questions about the subjects you are studying, your career plans and your non-academic interests. Any offer of a place is likely to be conditional on your obtaining specified grades in examinations to be taken prior to entering the course.

An employee selection interview is likely to be much more formal. You are likely to be interviewed by middle-aged people who, after years of experience, have reached positions of responsibility. Your appearance and attitude will be as important as what you say. Your dress and language should be appropriate for the occasion; and you must not arrive late.

The people you meet before and during the interview are selling themselves and their organisation: their appearance and attitude make an impression on you – just as yours does on them. They want to appoint suitable employees and to place them in appropriate work. As well as asking questions, they should ensure (either before or during the interview) that the applicant is aware of the working conditions, job requirements, working hours and pay scales.

When the time comes for the interview, walk confidently into the room. Do not sit until you are invited to do so. Sit upright so that your clothes look good and you feel comfortable, self-confident and alert.

Conversation is likely to be formal at first but a good interviewer will make any necessary introductions and help you to feel at ease. In a short time, from your qualifications and experience, the work you have done previously, and your other interests (as indicated by your application, the comments of referees, and their impressions during the interview) the interviewers have to decide: (a) how interested you are, how enthusiastic, and how well qualified; (b) how successful you have been in any previous employment; (c) how well you present yourself and how well you communicate during the interview; (d) how well you are likely to do the kind of work for which you have applied, or fill the particular vacancy they have in mind; and (e) how well you are likely to get on with other employees and, if necessary, with customers.

When meeting people for the first time it is not usually possible to judge their honesty, loyalty, persistence or reliability. But it is possible to get an impression of their appearance, alertness, attitudes, forcefulness, interests, manners. Table 10.1 is an example of the kind of assessment form some interviewers use, in employment interviews, in an attempt to make an objective comparison of applicants.

Answering questions

The questioning will not be aggressive: the interviewer's intention is to recruit suitable employees – not to put them off. You may be asked, first, questions based on details given in your application. These require a concise reply, but more than just 'Yes' or 'No'. Giving brief answers to such factual questions gives you time to relax a little. Speak clearly and use your normal speaking voice. As in normal conversation, look at anyone asking you a question, and make eye contact with all those you are addressing. Do not be afraid to smile occasionally. In other words, show your interest in the questions you are asked and in everyone present.

Listen carefully to the questions, and try to give short and straightforward answers to any simple questions. A quick response might be taken to indicate a lively mind, but do not feel that you have to respond immediately to every question. If you need a few moments for thought before answering, allow yourself time to think.

If asked for an opinion, say what you think and then, briefly, say why – to make clear that you are expressing a considered and well-founded view. Try to summarise your thoughts when a question calls for a longer

Table 10.1 Interviewer's record and applicant-rating form/applicant's check list

Trait	Assessment			
1 *Appearance*	Unfavourable	Suitable	Favourable	Impressive
2 *Speech*	Indistinct	Clear	Pleasant	Good
3 *Attitude*	Unapproachable	Friendly	Likeable	Inspiring
4 *Alertness*	Misunderstands	Slow	Quick	Bright
5 *Stability*	Impatient	Balanced	Calm	In control
6 *Knowledge of subject*	Inadequate	Satisfactory	Good	Outstanding
7 *Answers*	Confused	Involved	Clear	Convincing
8 *Judgement*	Impulsive	Balanced	Good	Inspiring
9 *Confidence*	Withdrawn	Hesitant	Confident	Self-assured
10 *Character*	Insincere	Frank	Sincere	Likeable
11 *Knowledge of business*	Lacking	Superficial	Evident	Exceptional
12 *Interest in vacancy*	Uninterested	Not evident	Interested	Enthusiastic

Summary

Strengths:

Weaknesses:

Suitability for course/employment:

Note
This is an example of the kind of form used in some employment interviews. The traits listed, and the weighting of each trait on any rating scale in an attempt to be objective, should depend on the kind of work for which applicants are being considered.

reply, so that you do not talk for too long at a time. Interviewers can ask further questions if they require more detail.

If you write on the application form, or in your *curriculum vitae*, that you have certain interests, you must be ready to answer relevant questions. Your answers will indicate the extent of your interest – and how enthusiastic you are. So look through your application when you are preparing for the interview. This should help you to expect certain questions and be ready to reply. If you are a student applying for your first permanent position, you could be asked questions about a project you completed as part of your course or how you feel you benefited from any vacation employment. Be prepared to talk about anything mentioned on your *curriculum vitae* that could invite comment or need further explanation.

Volunteering important information

Be prepared, during the interview, to take opportunities to draw attention to those interests and experiences that you particularly wish the interviewer or the interviewing panel to know about. Do not assume that everyone present has read, and considered carefully, every word of your application; or that the relevance of your previous experience to the post for which you are applying is obvious to everyone. Emphasise your skills and achievements which are relevant to the questions you are answering, even though these are clearly stated in your application for the post.

In speaking about others, for example your present employer, bear in mind that everyone appreciates praise, and that if you cannot say anything good about anyone it is usually best to say nothing at all.

Behaving naturally

Present your true personality. An employer's selection procedures are an attempt to recruit people who will contribute to the success of the business, and may place great emphasis on the ability to work as part of a team.

However, it is important that each individual should also be self-reliant and able to accept responsibilities. Indeed, some people will be most effective when allocated a task and left to consult others only when they consider it necessary.

In this connection, Albert Einstein described himself as 'a horse for single harness, not cut out for team work'. There is something wrong with a selection procedure if too much emphasis is placed on the ability to work as part of a team. It would be regrettable if suitable people were to be excluded simply because an interviewer thought they would work best on their own, think for themselves, and be prepared to speak their minds.

Asking questions

Ask questions during the interview if they fit into the conversation. For example, you might need to ask for clarification before you could answer a question or you might have the opportunity to show your interest in a topic being discussed.

However, towards the end of the interview you will probably be asked if you have any questions. Be prepared for this. Before the interview, make a note of one or two questions that you would particularly like to ask. For example, you could ask about training opportunities and promotion prospects if these had not already been mentioned, or about anything else you needed to know that could help you to decide whether or not to accept the post if it were offered to you. If you have no questions you could say, for example: 'No thank you, the further particulars you provided were clear and my questions have already been answered when I visited the department' or, if appropriate, 'No thank you, but I am sure I should find the work interesting.'

Taking an oral examination

In some subjects, especially languages, oral or *viva voce* examinations are assessed (like any other practical examination); but in most subjects they provide the external examiner with the opportunity (a) to meet students who have, after assessment, been assigned to different grades; and (b) in some institutions to explore the strengths and weaknesses of those students whose marks are just below the borderline between grades, and consider whether or not any of them could be reconsidered and awarded the higher grade. But students would probably be assured, before such an interview, that although they could be up-graded on the advice of an external examiner they would not be down-graded.

Oral examinations are also used in the assessment of candidates for the award of higher degrees, to allow an external examiner to ask questions about work completed and reported in a dissertation or thesis.

In any oral examination you must be prepared to talk about your subject. The examiner, having looked at your written answers to examination questions and at any extended essay or project report (completed as part of your work for a first degree), dissertation or thesis (based on your studies for a first or for a higher degree), will want to discuss your work.

Your oral examination is an opportunity to impress. Dress appropriately to meet the examiner. In the interview, an experienced examiner will help you to feel at ease. It is good that you should feel keyed up and ready for action, as anyone would before a talk (see pages 89, 100), but having prepared well you should also feel self-confident and ready to speak for yourself.

Walk confidently into the room. The examiner will probably stand to greet you and indicate where you should sit. Sit upright so that you are comfortable but alert. The examiner will check your name, to make sure that you are the person expected at this time.

As in normal conversation, be polite and self-confident but not aggressive. Obviously, you will be taking the examination seriously but do smile occasionally: show your interest and enthusiasm for your subject.

Speak clearly. Try not to answer simply yes or no. Give more information or explanation to show your knowledge and understanding, but do not talk for too long in answer to any question. If necessary, the examiner can ask further questions on the same topic before moving on to something else.

When necessary, give yourself time to think: you do not need to answer every question immediately. A few moments of reflection may give you time to collect your thoughts and summarise your reply.

If you do not understand any question, or are not quite sure exactly what the examiner wants to know, do not be afraid to ask for clarification.

Counselling

Talking things over with someone you can trust may help you to review your progress in any employment and to decide how any problem may be tackled. Such conversations, with fellow students and with your tutor or other lecturers, should be a normal part of a review of progress and of mature reflection at each stage in any activity. Anyone can benefit from and should welcome constructive feedback.

However, there may be times when you need to discuss a problem with someone who is not connected with your work. This is why many large organisations (including colleges and universities) employ counsellors, trained to listen, to whom students or employees can speak *in confidence* about any personal problem that is adversely affecting their work. Just talking about a problem with someone whom you can trust, and whose judgement you respect, may help to relieve stress. Also, the counsellor is likely to have had experience of helping others with similar problems.

Counselling is a matter of helping others to find solutions to problems, not of solving the problems for them. Anyone with a problem can seek counselling; anyone who recognises that someone else has a problem (perhaps a fellow student) may suggest to the person concerned that a counsellor may be able to help.

The counsellor will be able to allocate time, free from interruptions, to talk in confidence. The counsellor will listen, talk about the nature of the problem, ask questions in seeking a fuller understanding, and may offer reassurance, provide information and encouragement, discuss possible courses of action, and offer support – including the opportunity for further meetings.

Bibliography

Most of the publications listed are referred to in the text. The notes after the bibliographic details of some works are to indicate their usefulness or their authors' intentions, where this is not clear from the title alone.

Baker, J. and Westrup, H. (2003) *Essential Speaking Skills: a Handbook for English Language Teachers*, London: Continuum. For anyone who organises courses on teaching English in schools and colleges, with suggestions for many exercises that can be undertaken with classes of any size and require few resources.

Barrass, R. (2001) *Study! A Guide to Effective Learning, Revision and Examination Techniques*, 2nd edn, London: Routledge.

Barrass, R. (2002) *Writing at Work: a Guide to Better Writing in Administration, Business and Management*, London: Routledge.

Barrass, R. (2005) *Students Must Write: a Guide to Better Writing in Course Work and Examinations*, 3rd edn, London: Routledge.

BBC (2005) *The Use of Body Language in Different Cultures*. BBC World Service. Available at http://www.bbc.uk/worldservice/learningenglish/business/wab [26 April 2005].

Bullock, A. (1975) *A Language for Life*, London: HMSO. Includes a forthright note of dissent by Stuart Froome, concerning the relationship between declining standards in the use of English by pupils and changes in teaching methods in the 1960s.

Burchfield, R. (1981) *The Spoken Word: a BBC Guide*, London: BBC.

Carnegie, D. (1988) *How to Win Friends and Influence People*, London: Heinemann. A textbook for courses on effective speaking or human relations (first published 1937) to help people in business and the professions develop their self-confidence and overcome their fears about speaking in public.

Churchill, W. S. (1897) 'The scaffolding of rhetoric', unpublished. Cambridge: Churchill Archives Centre, Churchill Papers, CHAR 08/013.

Cobbett, W. (1819) *A Grammar of the English Language, in a Series of Letters*, Providence, RI: John Doyle; 1923 edn reprinted 2002 by Oxford University Press, Oxford.

Crowley, T. (1989) *The Politics of Discourse*, Houndmills: Macmillan.

Dearing, R. (1997) *Higher Education in the Learning Society: Report of the National Committee of Inquiry into Higher Education*, London: HMSO.

DES (2005) *Educational Statistics First Release*, London, Department of Education and Skills.

DFE (1995) *English in the National Curriculum*, Department for Education, London: HMSO. Note: the general teaching requirements relating to the use of language across the curriculum are available at http://www.nc.uk.net/nc_resources.html/language.shtml [26 April 2005].

Dickens, C. (1850) *David Copperfield*, London: Chapman & Hall (London: Oxford University Press edn 1948).

Dickens, C. (1884) *Martin Chuzzlewit*, London: Chapman & Hall (Oxford University Press edn 1951.

EEC (1988) *Quality Standards for Cucumbers*, Brussels: Commission Regulation (EEC) No. 1677/88.

Flesch, R. F. (1962) *The Art of Plain Talk*, London and New York: Collier-Macmillan. Includes advice on writing as well as on speaking.

Forster, E. M. (1924) *A Passage to India*, London: Edward Arnold, 1946 edn.

Fowler, H. W. (1968) *A Dictionary of Modern English Usage*, 2nd edn revised E. Gowers, London: Oxford University Press.

Fowler, H. W. and Fowler, F. G. (1906) *The King's English*, Oxford: Clarendon Press.

Gowers, E. (1986) *The Complete Plain Words*, 3rd edn revised S. Greenbaum and J. Whitcut, London: HMSO.

Grimson, A. C. and Ramsaran, S. (1989) *An Introduction to the Pronunciation of English*, London: Edward Arnold.

Hardy, T. [1874] (1993) *Far from the Madding Crowd*, Oxford: Oxford University Press.

Jaques, D. (2000) *Learning in Groups*, 3rd edn, London: Kogan Page. A handbook for tutors and trainers, providing guidance on group organisation, and on group activities, monitoring and assessment, based mainly on the work of the Centre for Staff and Learning Development at the Oxford Brookes University.

Jay, A. (1993) *Effective Presentations*, London: Pitman (for Institute of Management).

Kingman, J. (1988) *Report of the Committee of Inquiry into the Teaching of English Language*, Department of Education and Science, London: HMSO. In which one member of the committee, Professor H. G. Widdowson, expresses his regrets that the committee does not clearly define English as a subject. See also Sampson (1925) in this list.

Laver, J. and Hutcheson, S., eds (1972) *Communication in Face to Face Interaction*, Harmondsworth: Penguin Books.

Mullen, J. (1997) 'Graduates deficient in "soft" skills', *People Management*, 3 (22): 18.

Napley, D. (1975) *The Technique of Persuasion*, 2nd edn, London: Sweet & Maxwell.

Newbolt, H. (1921) *The Teaching of English in England*, London: HMSO.

Orwell, G. (1946) 'Politics and the English language', *Horizon*, 76 (April); reprinted (1957) in *Selected Essays*, Harmondsworth: Penguin Books.

Post, E. (1942) *Etiquette: the Book of Social Usage*, New York: Funk & Wagnalls.

Potter, S. (1966) *Our Language*, 2nd edn, Harmondsworth: Penguin Books. A concise introduction to the origins of English words, to their use, to the development of English as an international language, and to sources of further information.

Quiller-Couch, A. (1906) *From a Cornish Window*, Bristol: Arrowsmith.

Quiller-Couch, A. (1916) *On the Art of Writing*, Cambridge: Cambridge University Press.

Reagans, R. W. (1990) *An American Life*, London: Hutchinson.

Roberts, D., ed. (1998) *Lord Chesterfield's Letters to His Son*, Oxford: Oxford University Press.

Ross, W. D., ed. (1946) *The Works of Aristotle*, 11, London: Oxford University Press.

Salmon, G. (2002) *E-tivities: the Key to Active Online Learning*, London: Kogan Page. Advice on planning, developing and supervising online activities.

Sampson, George (1925) *English for the English*, Cambridge: Cambridge University Press. Considers the impact of the Education Act of 1870 over fifty years, asserts the importance of teaching English to the English, and defines precisely what he considers should be the aim and content of the study of English.

Sillitoe, Alan (1961) *Key to the Door*, London: Macmillan.

Sprat, T. [1667] (1959) *History of the Royal Society*, London: Routledge & Kegan Paul.

Turk, C. (1985) *Effective Speaking: Communication in Speech*, London: E. & F. Spon. This research-based guide, intended mainly for people who have to give presentations as part of their work, includes bibliographic references to many original research papers.

Index